Energize Your Audience!

Energize Your Audience!

**75 Quick Activities
That Get Them
Started. . .
and Keep Them Going**

LORRAINE L. UKENS

JOSSEY-BASS/PFEIFFER
A Wiley Company
www.pfeiffer.com

Published by Pfeiffer
A Wiley Imprint
989 Market Street, San Francisco, CA 94103-1741   www.pfeiffer.com

ISBN: 0-7879-4530-7
Library of Congress Catalog Card Number 99-050575

Pfeiffer books and products are available through most bookstores. To contact Pfeiffer directly call our Customer Care Department within the U.S. at 800-956-7739, outside the U.S. at 317-572-3986, or fax 317-572-4002.

Pfeiffer also publishes its books in a variety of electronic formats. Some content that appears in print may not be available in electronic books.

Library of Congress Cataloging-in-Publication Data

Ukens, Lorraine L.
     Energize your audience : 75 quick actvities that get them started—
and keep them going / Lorraine L. Ukens.
        p.   cm.
Includes index.
     ISBN 0-7879-4530-7 (pbk. : alk. paper)
1. Adult learning. 2. Active learning. 3. Training. I. Title.
     LC5225.L42 U54 2000
     331.25'92—dc21   99-050575

Acquiring Editor: Matthew Holt
Director of Development: Kathleen Dolan Davies
Developmental Editor: Susan Rachmeler
Editor: Rebecca Taff
Senior Production Editor: Dawn Kilgore
Cover Design: Frani Halperin

Printed in the United States of America

Printing 10 9 8 7

To my daughter,

Kristina,

whose dedication to her art
is a constant source
of inspiration and pride.

Contents

Energizers

Group Challenges

About the Author

Introduction

You know the scenario: You're pressed for time, and you have a lot of content to cover. You know that you will need to spend some time helping your participants become acquainted with one another—and what about those lags in energy that seem to occur throughout the day, especially after lunch? You want to make the session active, but you cannot use those old stand-by activities you have stashed away because they take more time than you have available.

Energize Your Audience was written to help facilitators provide the icebreakers, energizers, and group challenges that are so critical to the active learning process; and all take fifteen minutes or less. These quick activities will get participants started and keep them going throughout training sessions or meetings. Have fun choosing!

Experiential Learning

Principles of Experiential Learning

Few of us can argue that experience is the richest resource for adult learning. Games and other hands-on activities can facilitate the learning process in a most innovative and enjoyable way, and people retain knowledge more easily when they experience a lesson in an unforgettable way. The idea is to put people in experiences that provide them with opportunities to become actively involved. Games serve to pull the learner into the center of the actual learning situation.

Experiential learning provides participants with a structured activity that contributes to both content and process goals. Also referred to as hands-on or action-based learning, the emphasis is on what participants do rather than on what they are told by the trainer. Learning occurs when a person engages in some activity, looks back on it critically, extracts some useful insight, then applies the concept to a real-life situation.

The outcomes of the activity are analyzed in relation to some learning objective(s) set into the design.

Benefits of Active Participation

Hands-on learning experiences help keep participants active, alert, and productive. When utilizing such activities, the facilitator must remember that adult learners share certain characteristics that may affect the overall training environment. First, they have strong feelings about learning situations in general. Because they have a good deal of first-hand experience, adults bring along a wealth of ideas to contribute to training events. They also have set habits and distinct beliefs that can affect their learning. Facilitators may need to develop a receptive environment to expand mind-sets and allow behavioral changes to occur.

Adult learners also have a great many preoccupations outside a practical learning situation, such as work waiting to be done or personal problems. To cope with possible overload, individuals develop selective stimuli filters that allow them to concentrate on the preferred data. Therefore, if participants are not stimulated by the learning situation, distractions may become the focal point for their attention. Active learning events requiring the involvement of all group members can help alleviate this problem.

It is important for employees to be provided with opportunities to rehearse new skills and behaviors by practicing them in a safe, low-risk environment. Experiential activities, when used properly and sensitively, can help allay many of the fears that are associated with the learning process and allow for a comfortable environment of discovery. Ultimately, this practice aids in the transfer of the new knowledge to the actual work environment.

Adult learners want to appear in control; therefore, they often display restricted emotional responses. Icebreakers and energizers can help break through that surface resistance. Using games in training programs helps take the participants' minds off pressure at work and diminishes their anxiety about learning new things or facing controversial issues. A fun approach also diminishes some of the distractions that many workers feel when they take time away for training. They often can relax and listen better if their stress is relieved and defensiveness broken down. Playful activities provide people with a shared history and better sense of how to relate to one another. For real learning to take place, emotions must be involved. What better way to do this than for everyone to be fully immersed in an activity?

Types of Experiences

All of the activities in this book will help to create high energy levels in training sessions and meetings. For ease of selection, they have been grouped into three categories: icebreakers, energizers, and group challenges. The purpose of each is given below.

Icebreakers
The main objective of this category is to have participants become acquainted and mix together. This helps support the early stages of the group's development as members build a sense of comfort, as well as a sense of belonging.

2

Energizers

The purpose of the activities in this category is to invigorate the participants and increase their attention levels. These are especially useful after breaks in the session or as transitional experiences when introducing new topics.

Group Challenges

Activities in this category are intended to promote group cohesion through participation in a group event. The activities are designed to challenge the physical or mental capabilities of the participants, and they require the joint efforts of group members to complete the assigned tasks.

Fundamentals

Choosing the Activity

Experiential activities and games must be used thoughtfully. They are not meant only as a means of having fun, but must be seen as a means to an end. Icebreakers, energizers, and group challenges can help pave the way for the main subject matter to follow, or they can be used to demonstrate a particular concept. Therefore, always choose an event that can be related to the theme or goal of the upcoming session. Activities can succeed with any subject matter, any segment of the workforce, and for most brief training sessions. However, the activity should always fit within the context of the whole instructional process. Because games are so flexible, they offer the opportunity to vary conditions in accordance with the needs of a specific group. Facilitators must be open to the possibility of varying the content or the process of the activity to meet the individual needs of groups, as well as any limits in material resources.

For any given learning objective, many different activities could be used, differing in complexity and in the demands made of the participants. Facilitators must select activities that are most suitable for the intended audience. Possible activities from which to choose encompass a wide variety that might involve such things as solving problems and puzzles, making self-disclosure statements, role playing, creating art objects, and so on. In addition, the activities may incorporate performing individually or in pairs, triads, small groups, or large groups. Be aware that the actual number of participants often limits the kind of activity that can be used; also be aware of any environmental factors that may restrict playing conditions.

Group Size and Time Required

In general, the activities presented here are very flexible in regard to group size and timing. The listed time required is only an approximation because the length of the activity depends on several variables: the number of participants, the extent and style of the debriefing, and so on. A general guideline to follow is that the larger the group, the longer the time required. This is not a hard-and-fast rule, but it is a rather good indicator of what happens in large groups, because the debriefing and reporting generally take longer.

Facilitator's Role

With experiential learning, the facilitator's role is to help the participants make the connection(s) between the experience and the intent of the learning. There must be a good match between the metaphors of the event and real-life issues. The activity itself must be set up, run, and processed properly, with a link to concrete situations in the real world.

The facilitator must emphasize the gravity of the instructional message, in addition to the fun, so that participants take the training seriously. Therefore, the debriefing is a critical point for making the connections to the real world of work. Debriefing is an art that must be interactive. The facilitator leads people to insights by discussing, reflecting, and questioning what was experienced. Rather than telling the participants the learning points of the activity, an effective facilitator guides them into realizations about what occurred.

Unless the activity calls for the facilitator to take an active role, the participants should be allowed to experience the event on their own. They should be allowed the freedom to make mistakes, because this in itself is an excellent way to analyze the situation and learn from the experience. Facilitators should intervene only on questions of procedure and only to give as much information as possible to clarify the situation without influencing the outcome.

Debriefing

The feedback session is the most important step in making the connection between the activity and what is to be learned from it. The questions that are presented with each activity are intended to help guide participants in seeing the relevance of the event within the context of the training session's objectives. They are by no means inclusive, and the facilitator should feel free to add others. In addition, feedback during the debriefing session may lead to other areas of discussion not specifically included here. This is especially true when "mistakes" have occurred during the actual event that may lead to new insights.

Summary

Games and other hands-on experiences can be one of the most innovative and enjoyable parts of any training course. They stimulate discussion and learning and help illustrate, emphasize, or summarize a point in a very effective way. Because of their flexible structure, such activities help meet a variety of learning styles and can be applied to a wide range of training topics.

The hands-on activities found here serve an important function. They encompass an audience-friendly approach that increases attention levels, keeps participants alert and productive, and boosts information retention. The icebreakers will help you, as the facilitator, get things started on the right foot; and the energizers and group challenges will help you maintain a sustained level of participation throughout the session. Training games can be just the right vehicle to motivate your participants to become actively involved in the learning process. And when learning becomes enjoyable, people develop the desire to comprehend even more.

4

Icebreakers

Animal Attraction

Objective

To uncover appropriate animal identities.

Time Required

Five to ten minutes.

Group Size

An unlimited number of participants, who will form pairs.

Materials

One prepared gummed label for each participant; pen or felt-tipped marker.

Preparation

Mark the gummed labels, one for each participant, with the name of a different animal. The labels should be created in pairs, for example, make two labels that say giraffe, two that say elephant, two that say rabbit, and so forth. (*NOTE:* If there will be an odd number of participants, make three labels for one kind of animal.)

Process

1. Place one label on the back of each participant.

2. Explain that each participant is to try to find out who he or she is by asking questions of others. A player may ask only ONE question of each participant, and the question must be phrased so that it can be answered by "yes" or "no." As players discover their designated animals, they are to form a line, in order *according to the height of the animal.* As each player enters the line he or she is to the find the appropriate animal partner and stand face to face.

3. Signal for the activity to begin. When all the animals have been identified and lined up, instruct each pair to spend one minute getting to know one another.

Variation

Use this format to review content matter by creating pairs of labels with key words or concepts. Have participants group together according to main subject topics and review the specific content.

Discussion

- What kinds of questions were helpful in finding out what you represented?
- Could you have found out this information without asking others? How?
- Was it difficult to line up according to height? Why or why not?
- In what similar ways do we gather necessary information on the job?

Breakout

Objective

To break balloons tied to the wrists of other players.

Time Required

Five minutes.

Group Size

An unlimited number of participants.

Materials

One round non-latex balloon for each participant; string; scissors; clock or timer.

Preparation

Fully inflate each balloon and then tie it off. Cut the string into 12-inch lengths and attach one strand to each balloon so that two ends hang free.

Process

1. Distribute one prepared balloon to each participant.

2. Direct each player to gain assistance in tying the balloon around one of his or her wrists. The balloon should be tied tightly so that it fits snugly.

3. Explain that players are to try to push their balloons against other players' balloons in order to break the other person's without breaking their own. The goal is to be the only player remaining with an unbroken balloon.

4. Signal for the activity to begin. Allow approximately five minutes to pass, then stop the participants. Determine those participants whose balloons were not broken and congratulate them as the winners.

Discussion

- How did you feel during this activity?
- If the game were played again, what new rule(s) would you add? Why?
- Did you try to cooperate or compete with other players? Why?
- How does this relate to situations in the workplace?

Color My World

Objective

To attempt to match a color choice with a partner.

Time Required

Five minutes.

Group Size

An unlimited number of participants, who will work in pairs.

Materials

None.

Preparation

None.

Process

1. Instruct the participants to form pairs, facing one another.

2. Explain that you will conduct a game similar to the old favorite, "Rock, Paper, Scissors," except that participants will choose to say one of three colors. Say that, upon hearing the announcement, "1, 2, 3, Color!," each person is to look at his or her partner and simultaneously say one of the following colors: "red," "white," or "blue." This process is to be repeated every time you make the announcement. The object is to see how many times the partners can match their individual choices.

3. Make the announcement, "1, 2, 3, Color!"; then wait a few seconds and repeat the statement. Repeat this process several times.

4. Have the participants change partners and conduct the procedure again. Repeat the sequence as many times as desired.

Discussion

- How long did it take for you to begin to get "in sync" (synchronized) with your partner?

- How does a person's individual style of behavior affect interpersonal encounters?

- In what ways can we associate this activity with our work situations?

Date Line

Objective

To arrange temporary discussion partners. (*NOTE:* These worksheets can provide a structured format for later formation of partners when participants need to share information or discuss topics.)

Time Required

Fifteen minutes.

Group Size

Fifteen to thirty participants.

Materials

One copy of the Date Line Worksheet and a pencil for each participant; list of topics and time; clock or timer.

Preparation

Create a list of topics, followed by a whole-hour time designation. Choose topics that will allow participants to get to know one another and are non-threatening, for example, favorite food, hobby, TV show, and so forth.

Process

1. Distribute one copy of the Date Line Worksheet and a pencil to each participant. Direct the participants to write their names on the worksheets.

2. Explain that each participant is to locate a partner for each of the time slots on his or her clock. For example, if a participant has an opening at one o'clock, he or she would find someone else who also had an opening at one o'clock so that they could become partners. Tell participants that, as they form each partnership, they are to write each other's names on the clocks at the specified hour and to continue until all time slots have been filled. Announce that participants will have three minutes in which to complete this task.

3. Signal for the activity to begin, then time it for three minutes. Give a thirty-second warning, stopping the activity when time expires.

4. Explain that participants now will use their sheets to find partners to discuss a variety of assigned topics. As each topic and time slot is announced, participants are to find the person whose name appears on the line next to that time. At your signal, a new topic and time will be announced and participants are to move on to discuss the new topic with the partner designated for that time slot.

5. Using the prepared list, announce a topic and a time designation. Allow several minutes for discussion before announcing a new topic and time slot. Repeat this process as many times as desired.

6. Tell the participants to save their worksheets for use when partners are needed for sharing information or discussing other topics during the session.

Discussion

- Did you find more similarities or more differences between yourself and your partners?

- What were some unusual things you found out about some of your partners?

- How does diversity impact the ability of a team to perform effectively?

Date Line Worksheet

Name:

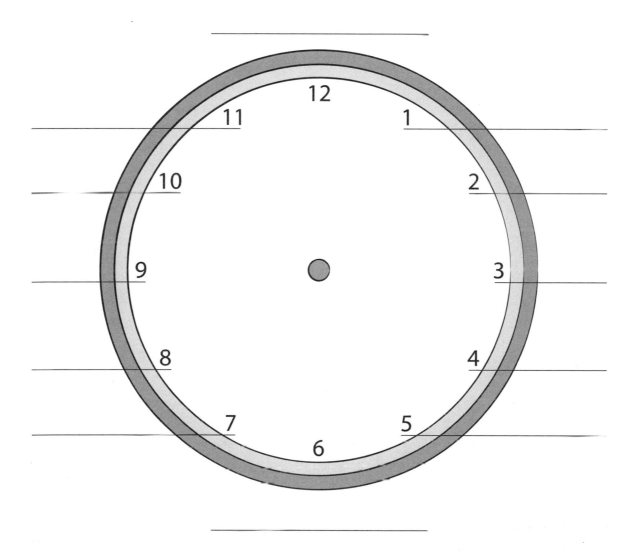

Following Procedures

Objective

To determine the identity of a procedure from a written description.

Time Required

Five to ten minutes.

Group Size

An unlimited number of participants.

Materials

One copy of the Following Procedures Worksheet and a pencil for each participant.

Preparation

None.

Process

1. Explain that each participant will receive the same description of a particular procedure. Based on the information received, each person should write a guess as to the identity of the procedure on the worksheet. Next, participants are to locate others who share the same answer and form small groups.

2. Distribute one copy of the Following Procedures Worksheet and a pencil to each participant.

3. Allow several minutes for participant interactions to occur. Stop the activity when you observe that most have gathered into one or more groups.

4. Obtain feedback from the group(s) as to what the procedure is. If no one has guessed the correct procedure, provide the answer.

Solution

Doing laundry.

Discussion

- What in the written description made you guess the particular procedure that you did?

- In your interactions with others, did you question those who had different answers about how they arrived at their guesses? Why or why not?

- Did anyone change his or her original guess? Why or why not?

- How does this relate to the way that you usually interpret and use information at home or work?

Following Procedures Worksheet

The procedure is actually quite simple. First, you arrange things into different groups. Of course, one pile may be sufficient depending on how much there is to do. If you have to go somewhere else due to lack of facilities, then that is the next step. Otherwise, you are fairly well set.

It is important not to overdo things. That is, it is better to do too few things at once than too many. In the short run, this may not seem important, but complications can easily arise. A mistake can be expensive as well. At first, the whole procedure will seem complicated. Soon, however, it will become just another fact of life. It is difficult to foresee any end to the necessity for this task in the immediate future, but one never can tell.

After the procedure is completed, one arranges the materials into groups again. Then they can be put into their appropriate places. Eventually, they will be used once again, and the whole cycle will have to be repeated. However, that is part of life!

What Procedure Am I?

For the Record

Objective

To create a record album cover representative of one's personal identity.

Time Required

Fifteen minutes.

Group Size

Five to twenty participants.

Materials

One square sheet of poster board (approximately one foot square) for each participant; several magazines, pairs of scissors, rolls of tape, bottles of glue, and colored felt-tipped markers; clock or timer.

Preparation

Place the magazines, scissors, tape, and markers in an area that is accessible to all participants.

Process

1. Distribute one sheet of poster board to each participant.

2. Explain that participants will use the poster board and other materials (indicate the available materials) to design a record album cover featuring themselves as the performers. Each album cover should reflect personal interests and/or qualities through its title, symbols, colors, and so forth. Items used may be drawn or may be cut out from the magazines provided. Announce that individuals will have ten minutes to complete their work.

3. Allow approximately ten minutes for individual work, then call time.

4. Have participants briefly share their album covers within groups of five each or with the large group, if time allows.

Discussion

- Why did you choose particular items to describe yourself?
- What qualities do you have that you feel are important?
- How does self-awareness impact an individual's ability to perform a job?

Hand-Off

Objective

To perform a series of hand greetings with various partners.

Time Required

Five minutes.

Group Size

An unlimited number of participants, who will work in rotating pairs.

Materials

One copy of the Hand-Off Directions Sheet for the facilitator.

Preparation

None.

Process

1. Direct the participants to stand scattered throughout the room.

2. Explain that the participants will engage in a fast-moving activity that will involve a series of partner "challenges" through which they will meet and interact with one another. Demonstrate the following actions with one of the participants:

   • Shake hands

   • High five (open-palm slap in the air with one hand)

   • Low five (open-palm slap at or below waist level with one hand)

   • High ten (open-palm slap in the air with both hands)

   Each time an instruction is called, participants are to find partners and perform the act, as they are introducing themselves to their partners.

3. Using the Hand-Off Directions Sheet, read the instructions to the participants. Announce each one, allowing several seconds for the interaction to take place before announcing the next one. Keep the pace fairly brisk.

Discussion

   • How did you feel during the activity? Why?

   • In what ways can we relate this activity to the workplace?

Hand-Off Directions Sheet

1. Choose a partner and   SHAKE HANDS.

2. Choose a new partner and   GIVE A "HIGH FIVE."

3. Find your original partner and   SHAKE HANDS.

4. Find your second partner and   GIVE A "HIGH FIVE."

5. Choose a new partner and   GIVE A "LOW FIVE."

6. Find your original partner and   SHAKE HANDS.

7. Find your second partner and   GIVE A "HIGH FIVE."

8. Find your third partner and   GIVE A "LOW FIVE."

9. Choose a new partner and   GIVE A "HIGH TEN."

10. Find your original partner and   SHAKE HANDS.

11. Find your second partner and   GIVE A "HIGH FIVE."

12. Find your third partner and   GIVE A "LOW FIVE."

13. Find your fourth partner and   GIVE A "HIGH TEN."

14. Find your original partner and   SHAKE HANDS.

Individual Choice

Objective

To guess the order of importance for a partner's list of personal descriptors.

Time Required

Ten to fifteen minutes.

Group Size

Twelve to fifty participants, who will work in pairs.

Materials

Two 5" x 7" index cards and a pencil for each participant; clock or timer.

Preparation

None.

Process

1. Distribute two 5" x 7" index cards and a pencil to each participant.

2. Using one card, have each participant write the numbers one through five, then list five personal things about himself or herself. Allow approximately three minutes to complete the task.

3. Using the second card, have each participant write the numbers one through five. Next, each is to rank the five items from the first card, in the order listed, with "1" as *most important to the person* to "5" as *least important to the person*. Allow approximately three minutes to complete this task.

4. Instruct the participants to pair up. Each pair is to exchange only the cards that list the five items, not revealing their ranking.

5. Direct the participants to take turns trying to guess their partners' ranking of the items.

Discussion

- Which participants learned something new about their partners? What did you learn?

- How close did you come to guessing your partner's ranking of items correctly?

- What observations about your partner influenced you to guess the order you did?

- How does personal perception influence our relationships with others?

Let's Mingle

Objective

To interact with other participants based on outward appearance.

Time Required

Five minutes.

Group Size

An unlimited number of participants, who will work in rotating groups of four or five.

Materials

None.

Preparation

None.

Process

1. Explain that the purpose of the activity is to simply walk around among others in the group while saying, "Mingle, mingle, mingle" until you give a command. Participants who share a similar detail of the command will gather in groups of four or five and introduce themselves, then discuss their favorite hobbies.

2. Signal for the participants to start mingling. After a few moments, give a command from one of those listed below, or make up your own.

hair color	color of shoes	color of shirt
wearing glasses	wearing a watch	age
height	length of hair	gender

3. Continue with four or five mingles or until you are ready to form groups for the next activity. If you want an exact number in each group for another activity, your last command will be, "groups of five," for example.

Discussion

- What kinds of assumptions do we make based on outward appearances?
- What did you find out about other people through your group discussions?
- Were your initial assumptions compatible with the information you obtained?
- How does what happened in this activity relate to the workplace?

Like a Rock

Objective

To locate individual pebbles from a larger group.

Time Required

Ten to fifteen minutes.

Group Size

Ten to thirty participants.

Materials

One pebble or small stone for each participant, plus a few extra.

Preparation

Collect pebbles or small stones that are all about the same size but with distinctive features, either in shape or surface texture.

Process

1. Distribute one pebble to each participant.

2. Explain that each participant is to study all the pebble's characteristics so that he or she knows it well enough to identify it by touch only, without looking at it. Allow a few minutes for observation and exploration.

3. Instruct the participants to form groups of two or three. Members of each group are to describe their pebbles and swap them to see the differences. Allow a few minutes for this to occur.

4. Instruct each small group to combine with another one to form a larger group of four to six participants. Members of these groups are to sit in a circle with all the pebbles in a pile in front of a leader. Explain that, upon your signal, the leader will pass the pebbles, one at a time, so that each circulates around the group. Each individual is to try to find his or her own pebble with eyes closed.

5. Tell participants to close their eyes. Signal for the leaders to pass the pebbles around in their groups. Allow several minutes for individuals to locate their pebbles, then stop the activity and tell participants to open their eyes. Ask how many were able to locate the correct pebble.

6. Instruct all the groups to combine into a large circle. Explain that individuals will again attempt to locate their own pebbles from a collection of all the pebbles, following the previous procedure. Collect all the pebbles, tell participants to close their eyes, then pass the pebbles, one by one, around the group. Continue until each person has selected a stone. (*NOTE:* For larger groups, this step may be eliminated.)

Discussion

- How many of you were able to locate the correct pebble?
- How much of your success in locating your pebble was due to your ability to observe? How much was due to perception?
- How can we relate this activity to the uniqueness of each individual?

Pick Your Partner

Objective

To differentiate between true and false statements relating to others.

Time Required

Ten minutes.

Group Size

Ten to fifty participants, who will work in rotating pairs.

Materials

Five toothpicks for each participant.

Preparation

None.

Process

1. Distribute five toothpicks to each participant.
2. Explain that the goal of this activity is to collect as many toothpicks as possible by using the power of perception.
3. Explain that each participant is to challenge another person to disclose some piece of information about himself or herself. The challenger will then determine whether the information that is given is true or false. If the challenger guesses correctly, he or she takes one toothpick from the other person. If the challenger is not correct, the other person takes one toothpick from the challenger. Once this exchange has taken place, the roles are reversed with the current partner; then new partners are chosen and the process continues until time is called.
4. Announce that the activity is to begin. Allow five to ten minutes to elapse before calling time.
5. Determine who has the most toothpicks and provide a prize to this "most perceptive" participant.

Discussion

- Was this task difficult? Why or why not?
- How does perception affect an individual's view of the world?
- What impact does perception have in the workplace?

Rave Reviews

Objective

To disclose information on individual experiences.

Time Required

Ten to fifteen minutes.

Group Size

An unlimited number of participants, who will work in groups of three.

Materials

Clock or timer.

Preparation

None.

Process

1. Instruct the participants to form groups of three members each.

2. Explain that, upon your signal, each person is to take a turn to share with the two partners the high point and the low point of his or her life *during the past week,* that is, tell what was most satisfying and what was least satisfying. Announce that the triads will have five minutes in which to complete this task.

3. Allow a few moments for participants to think, then signal for the activity to begin. Time the groups for five minutes. Stop the discussion and ask the participants to focus on the process that just occurred. Conduct a discussion, based on the questions in the Discussion section below.

4. You may end the activity here, or you may wish to repeat the procedure with a new topic. Some suggested topics include:

   • Tell about a turning point in your career (life).

   • Share something about a hero of yours, either living or dead.

   • Tell about the person who has had the most impact on your life.

   • Describe some things you do that you think are unconventional.

5. Ask participants the same discussion questions to see whether the process changed.

Discussion

   • Did you feel that others really listened to you? Why or why not?

   • Did you openly share your feelings or did you screen them before talking about them? Why?

   • Would you have added anything to your discussion if you had had more time? Why or why not?

   • How does this activity relate to your other interpersonal relationships?

Roving Reporters

Objective

To conduct personal interviews with other participants.

Time Required

Ten to fifteen minutes.

Group Size

Ten to thirty participants, who will work in rotating pairs.

Materials

None.

Preparation

None.

Process

1. Instruct the participants to form pairs in a random way and to introduce themselves to one another.

2. Direct the pairs to ask each other three simple, personal questions, for example, likes, dislikes, hobbies, interests, job, family, and so forth. Emphasize that each interviewer should make mental note of the responses. Allow several minutes for the exchange to occur.

3. Signal for the participants to change partners, introduce themselves, and alternate asking the three questions. Emphasize that each interviewer should make mental note of the responses. Allow several minutes for the exchange.

4. After several rotations of partners, direct all the participants to gather into a large circle.

5. Proceeding around the circle, one at a time, have each person give his or her name; then ask other participants to share information from their interviews with that person. Continue until all participants have been introduced.

Discussion

- What type of questions did interviewers ask?
- How well did your interviewers remember information about you?
- How does this activity relate to situations in which you meet someone for the first time?

Shake Down

Objective

To dispose of dried beans as you shake hands with others.

Time Required

Ten minutes.

Group Size

Ten to thirty participants.

Materials

Ten dried beans and one envelope per player; clock or timer.

Preparation

Prepare one envelope containing ten dried beans for each participant.

Process

1. Distribute one envelope of beans to each participant.

2. Explain that, upon a signal from you, the participants are to start shaking hands with one another, repeating the process over and over, with as many different people as possible. Each player is to give away one bean to every *fifth* person he or she shakes hands with. The object is to get rid of all the beans quickly. However, while people are trying to get rid of their beans, they are receiving beans from others. Emphasize that no one can refuse to accept a bean if he or she is really the fifth person whose hand is being shaken. Play will continue until time is called.

3. Signal for the activity to begin and allow approximately five minutes to elapse before calling time.

4. Have participants count the number of beans in their possession.

5. Declare a winner(s) by determining which player(s) had the smallest number of beans when time was called.

Variation

Play this game in exactly the opposite way; the one who ends up with the most beans is the winner.

Discussion

- How did you feel during the activity?
- How cooperative were other participants?
- How does this activity relate to various situations in the workplace?

Spin a Yarn

Objective

To "tie" group members into a cohesive unit through praising one another.

Time Required

Five to ten minutes.

Group Size

Five to thirty participants, who will work in groups of five to ten. (This activity works best with an intact work team or when participants are familiar with one another.)

Materials

One ball of yarn for each team.

Preparation

None.

Process

1. Instruct the participants to form groups of five to ten members each, standing in a circle. Allow sufficient space between groups.

2. Distribute one ball of yarn to one member of each group.

3. Explain that this is an exercise in praising members of a team. The person with the yarn is to toss the ball to someone else on the team and make a positive statement in the second person; for example, "Mary, you have a great sense of humor," or "John, thank you for helping me with my last project." The person receiving the compliment is to take up the slack, hold the string, then throw the ball of yarn to another team member, complimenting him or her. The team is to continue until all members have been included, then remain holding the yarn until further instructions.

4. Signal for teams to begin. After all members of the teams have received the yarn, ask them to examine the pattern formed and to note the ties that bind them together as a team.

5. Have the last person to receive the yarn in each team slowly roll up the ball while others let go of the yarn as needed.

Discussion

- Did the pattern formed by the yarn reveal specific team relationships? What was revealed?

- Were any of you surprised by a compliment you received? Why or why not?

- How do recognition and praise among team members help tie a group together?

- What are some concrete things that your team can do to become more cohesive at work?

Take Note

Objective

To locate players possessing an identical musical note.

Time Required

Ten minutes.

Group Size

Twenty-five to fifty participants, who will form seven groups.

Materials

One prepared musical note for each participant; scissors and a felt-tipped marker; radio music *(optional)*.

Preparation

Duplicate enough copies of the Take Note Template on card stock to accommodate one musical note shape for each participant. (Each sheet will provide two shapes.) Cut out each shape. Use the felt-tipped marker to mark each shape with one of the following notes of the music scale, alternating through the entire scale before repeating: *DO, RE, MI, FA, SO, LA, TI.* For example:

Process

1. Distribute the paper musical notes, one to each person. (If desired, use a radio to play some background music.)

2. Explain that, at a given signal, everyone is to hunt for other players who have the same note. Participants may sing their notes to attract their partners, if they wish.

3. Signal for the participants to begin.

4. When all the groups have assembled, announce that each group is to choose a song that it will sing, using only its own note instead of the words. The other groups will try to identify the song being presented. Allow a few minutes for the groups to choose their songs.

5. Have each group, in turn, present its song. Ask the other groups for their guesses as to the titles of the songs.

Discussion

- How did members of your group feel about performing the song?
- Did individual reactions impact the performance of the group as a whole? In what ways?
- How can we relate the saying "Birds of a feather flock together" to situations in the real world?

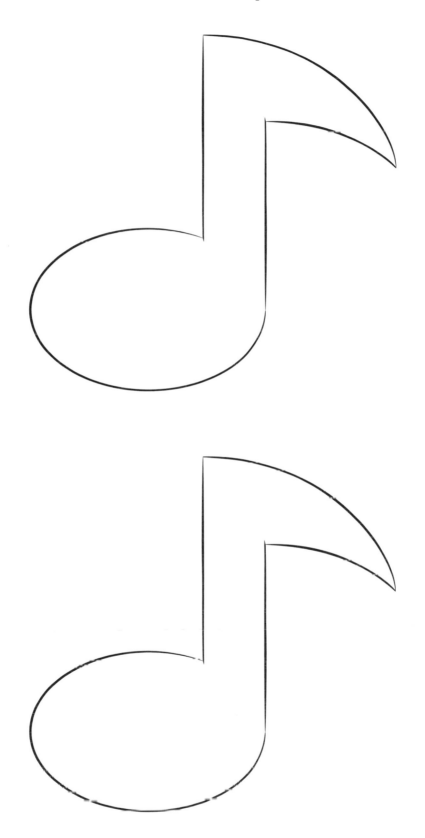

3, 2, 1, Contact!

Objective

To discover unusual facts that people have in common.

Time Required

Five to ten minutes.

Group Size

An unlimited number of participants, who will work in groups of three.

Materials

Clock or timer.

Preparation

None.

Process

1. Instruct the participants to form groups of three members each.

2. Explain that, upon a signal, members of each group of three will have two minutes to discover one *unusual* fact they share in common. Emphasize that the common item should be very specific (for example, all were born in the same state).

3. Signal for the activity to begin, then call time after two minutes.

4. Ask for examples of the unusual facts that were discovered.

5. Direct the participants to form new groups of three members each and to repeat the process. Continue this procedure as time allows.

Discussion

- Was this a difficult task? Why or why not?
- How do common interests provide a basis for establishing interpersonal relationships?
- How could common interests be used to create increased team cohesiveness?

Two by Two

Objective

To pair common items that are usually associated with each other.

Time Required

Five to fifteen minutes.

Group Size

Twelve to thirty participants, who will form pairs.

Materials

One set of paired items for every two participants; wrapping paper and tape. (*Variation: one paired picture set for every two participants; scissors.*)

Preparation

Collect things that are usually thought of as being used together: for example, cup and saucer, fork and knife, pen and pencil, nut and bolt, needle and thread, brush and comb, lock and key, envelope and stamp. Wrap each item separately.

Process

1. Explain that each person will receive an item that is generally associated with one other item that is in the possession of another participant. Each player is to find the other half of his or her pair.

2. Distribute one wrapped parcel to each player.

3. Signal for the activity to begin, then stop when all the appropriate pairs have formed.

4. You may wish to have the partners discuss an appropriate topic or perform an assigned task that is related to your lesson.

Variation

Collect representative pictures of paired items or use the picture cards provided on the Two by Two Worksheets 1 and 2 in place of the actual items. (*NOTE:* The worksheets provide enough sets for up to twenty-four participants.) Prepare the pictures on card stock and distribute one to each participant.

Discussion

- How can we relate this activity to the old adage, "Birds of a feather flock together"?
- What impact does this concept have in the workplace?

Two by Two Worksheet 1

Two by Two Worksheet 2

Wanted

Objective

To make "Wanted" posters representing individual personalities.

Time Required

Fifteen minutes.

Group Size

Five to twenty participants.

Materials

Personal pictures; one sheet of poster board (approximately 8" x 10") and a felt-tipped marker for each participant; tape or push pins; clock or timer.

Preparation

This requires advance contact with participants, requesting that each one bring in a picture of himself or herself (current, childhood, or baby).

Process

1. Distribute one sheet of poster board and a felt-tipped marker to each participant.

2. Explain that each participant is to use his or her personal picture to make a "Wanted" poster. Using Old West Wanted posters as an example, participants are to list some *negative* features, any aliases, where they are known to "hang out," and a reward for locating them.

3. Allow approximately ten minutes for individual work, then call time.

4. Have participants briefly share their posters within groups of five members each or with the large group, if time allows. Direct the participants to display the posters around the room.

Discussion

- Was it difficult to choose *negative* personal qualities to share with others? Why or why not?

- Did you learn anything new about people in the group? What did you learn?

Who Am I?

Objective

To identify a partner through descriptive adjectives.

Time Required

Ten to fifteen minutes.

Group Size

Twelve to forty participants; an even number of participants is required.

Materials

One 5" x 7" index card and a pencil for each participant; an empty shoe box.

Preparation

None.

Process

1. Distribute one 5" x 7" index card and a pencil to each participant.

2. Instruct each participant to write five adjectives describing himself or herself on the index card. *No names are to be written on the cards.* Emphasize that the information will be shared with other members of the group.

3. Allow approximately three minutes for individual work. Collect the cards and place them into the empty shoe box.

4. Direct participants to draw out one card each, making sure that they have not drawn their own cards.

5. Explain that each participant is to try to find the person whose card he or she has drawn. When a person is found, the participant is to have the person sign his or her name on the card.

6. Allow several minutes for the participants to mingle and find the card owners. When all owners have been located, have each participant introduce the person he or she found, reading aloud the adjectives written on the card.

Discussion

- How did you feel when your card was being shared? How many other people felt that same way?

- Why did you feel that way?

- How do your feelings and reactions influence personal performance on the job?

Energizers

All Dressed Up

Objective

To have each member receive one item as a bag of accessories is passed around the group.

Time Required

Five to ten minutes.

Group Size

Ten to twenty participants.

Materials

One large paper shopping bag with handles; at least one clothing accessory (such as hats, gloves, scarves, ear muffs, and so forth) for each participant, plus several additional pieces; timer.

Preparation

Place the clothing articles in the shopping bag.

Process

1. Instruct the participants to form a large circle.

2. Give the filled shopping bag to a player. Explain that, on your signal, he or she is to start rapidly passing the bag to the left and that the passing should continue around the group until the timer goes off. Whoever is holding the bag at that time must reach in and select one of the items to put on. This process will continue until the bag is empty. The goal is for everyone in the group to wear at least one item.

3. Set the timer for approximately one minute, and signal for the player to begin passing the bag. Once the person holding the bag removes an article and puts it on, reset the timer and signal once again for the bag to be passed.

4. Continue the process until all the clothing accessories have been removed from the bag. Determine how many, if any, group members did not receive an item.

Discussion

- How did you feel during the activity?
- Was it difficult trying to have each member of the group obtain an item? Why?
- How does this activity relate to teamwork in general? To your work on the job?

Another Point of View

Objective

To print one's name by focusing on its reflected image.

Time Required

Five minutes.

Group Size

Five to twenty participants.

Materials

One 8½" x 11" sheet of paper for every two participants; one pocket mirror and pencil for each participant; scissors.

Preparation

Cut each sheet of paper into half so that each participant has one half-sheet (8½" x 5½").

Process

1. Distribute one pocket mirror, one half-sheet of paper, and a pencil to each participant.

2. Direct the participants to fold the paper they receive in half lengthwise.

3. With the double edge of the paper at the top and the fold at the bottom, tell the participants to print their first names in capital letters on the side of the paper facing them.

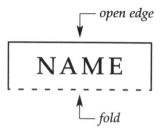

4. Direct the participants to flip their papers completely over to the blank side with the double edge at the bottom and the fold is at the top. Then they are to place the mirror near the top edge of the paper, above the fold, facing them.

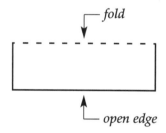

5. Tell the participants that they are to print their first names on the blank side of the paper while *keeping their eyes on the mirror ONLY.*

6. Allow several minutes for the participants to complete the task, then stop the activity.

7. Direct the participants to unfold the paper so that both printed names are revealed. Tell the participants to compare the two versions.

Discussion

- How did you feel while you were attempting this task?
- Why was it hard to write your name the second time?
- How can you relate this to the concept of change? To your perceptions?

By the Numbers

Objective

To create the highest consecutive number of "collections."

Time Required

Fifteen minutes.

Group Size

Ten to sixty participants, who will work in groups of five to eight.

Materials

Clock or timer. (*Optional:* A variety of common objects, such as buttons, pencils, plastic spoons, paper clips, or safety pins.)

Preparation

You may wish to distribute a variety of common objects throughout the room so that participants can locate necessary items easily.

Process

1. Instruct the participants to form groups of five to eight members each.

2. Explain that the object is for each group to create collections of similar objects in their possession,* in ascending consecutive number sequence. A group will begin with locating a single item, then two similar items, and on to three, four, and so forth. For example, a group creates the following collections: one ruler, two sticks of gum, three pencils, four matches, five pieces of paper, six pennies, and seven paper clips. The group must complete the appropriate number of the sequence before moving on to creating a collection of the next size. The winning group will be the one reaching the highest consecutive number of "collections." Announce that groups will have approximately five minutes to complete the task.

3. Signal for the groups to begin. Stop the activity after approximately five minutes (you may give groups more time if they are still actively engaged in the process).

4. Declare the winner by determining which group reached the highest number.

Discussion

- Was this task difficult to perform? Why or why not?
- Did group members have similar objects in their possession?
- How creative was your group in developing its "collections"?
- How does this activity relate to the use of available resources in the workplace?

*NOTE: If you have distributed items throughout the room, you may choose to announce that participants may use these in creating their collections or you may remain silent about the objects to see whether the items are utilized.

Calculated Terms

Objective

To calculate answers to a series of verbal equations mentally.

Time Required

Ten minutes.

Group Size

An unlimited number of participants.

Materials

One copy of the Calculated Terms Directions Sheet for the facilitator; one sheet of paper and a pencil for each participant.

Preparation

None.

Process

1. Distribute one sheet of paper and a pencil to each participant. Direct participants to write the numbers 1 through 10 on their papers.

2. Explain that you will read, aloud, a series of mathematical equations. The participants are to listen carefully to each question and do all calculations mentally, writing only the answers down on their papers.

3. One by one, read the statements found on the Calculated Terms Directions Sheet at a normal rate of speech. Pause *briefly* after each statement to allow the participants to write their answers.

4. Tell the participants to score their papers as you provide the answers below.

Solution

1. 36	4. 56	7. 18	9. 6
2. 4	5. 42	8. 8	10. 3
3. 14	6. 23		

Discussion

- How well did you do on this exercise?
- How many of you stopped listening when you became confused or lost on a question?
- Have you had people seem to stop listening when you were giving instructions?
- What can be done to prevent this loss of attention or to encourage active listening?

Calculated Terms Directions Sheet

1. Add the series of numbers: 3, 6, 8, 7, 7, and 5.

2. Start with the number 10, double it, add 4, then divide by 6.

3. From the number that is five times larger than 3, subtract 4, add 8, add 9, and divide by 2.

4. Double the sum of the numbers: 4, 6, 8, 5, 2, 3.

5. Subtract 13 from 20, add 14, divide by 3, multiply by 6.

6. For the series of numbers, 12, 8, 3, 5, 4, and 8, add the first three numbers.

7. Take half of the sum of the numbers, 4, 3, 8, and 5, then subtract 4, and multiply by 3.

8. Divide the number 56 by 7, divide by 4, add 12, and subtract 6.

9. Add the numbers, 8, 2, 7, and 4, then divide by 7, subtract 3, and add 6.

10. Take the square root of 16, add 5, divide by 3, add 9, and divide by 4.

Clear Reception

Objective

To provide quick feedback on transmitting descriptive messages.

Time Required

Fifteen minutes.

Group Size

Six to thirty participants, who will work in groups of three.

Materials

Magazines, calendars, old books, newspapers, and so forth; scissors; clock with second hand or stopwatch.

Preparation

For each group of three, cut at least three assorted pictures from the sources mentioned above.

Process

1. Instruct the participants to form groups of three members each. Within each group, one person is to be designated the sender, one the receiver, and one the observer.

2. Explain that the senders will be given a picture that neither the receiver nor the observer may see. The sender will have one minute to describe the contents of the picture to the other members of the group. At the end of the minute, the receiver will have one minute to recount the description he or she has heard. During this time, the observer will look at the picture and listen to the receiver's feedback. At the end of the receiver's minute, the receiver may look at the picture while the observer comments on the sending and receiving of the description.

3. Distribute one picture to the designated sender in each group, with the reminder to keep it hidden from the sender and observer.

4. Direct the senders to begin their descriptions, and time the activity for one minute. Stop the participants when time expires.

5. Direct the receivers to begin their feedback on the description, while observers look at the pictures and listen. Time for one minute, then stop the activity when time expires.

6. Direct the receivers to view the pictures while the observers provide their comments on the sending and receiving of the message.

7. Repeat the procedure described in Steps 3 through 6 until all group members have had the opportunity to send, receive, and observe.

Discussion

- How important was active listening in this activity?
- What types of discrepancies occurred between the message sent and the one received?
- How does this activity relate to communication in general?
- How can you apply what you have learned back on the job?

Clip-Clop-Plop

Objective

To pass signals around the group circle.

Time Required

Five minutes.

Group Size

Five to fifteen participants.

Materials

Clock or timer.

Preparation

None.

Process

1. Instruct the participants to form a large circle. Designate one person as the leader.

2. Explain that, on your signal, the leader will start the activity by pointing the index finger of one hand at the person on either his or her left or right and saying "CLIP. That person then goes next. This person can either repeat the action of the leader by pointing in the same direction and repeating the word "CLIP" or reverse the direction by pointing back in the direction from which he or she received the signal while saying "CLOP." The third possibility is that the second person can point at anyone in the circle and say "PLOP" and that person goes next. This process will continue until time is called.

3. Signal for the leader to begin. Time for approximately two to three minutes, then stop the activity.

Discussion

- How did you feel during this activity? Why?
- Was there any confusion in sending the signals? Why or why not?
- How do mixed messages affect our ability to communicate with others?

Close Calls

Objective

To pass several verbal messages at the same time.

Time Required

Ten minutes.

Group Size

Ten to twenty participants.

Materials

None.

Preparation

None.

Process

1. Instruct the participants to stand in a circle and count off alternately by "1" and "2."

2. Explain that the group will be passing several verbal messages at the same time. To begin, each "1" will whisper a message to the "2" on his or her right. Next, the "2s" will pass the messages along to the right so that many messages are being passed at once. The messages are to continue around the entire circle until they return to the originators.

3. Signal for the activity to begin. When the messages have completed the circuit, direct the players to share their messages in both the original and final versions.

Variation

Players stand in a line. The object is to pass two messages in opposite directions as follows: The person at each end of the line will whisper a message to the next person, who whispers it to the third person, and so on until the two messages reach the opposite ends of the line. The two end players will repeat the messages aloud and compare them to the original messages.

Discussion

- How similar to the original message was the final one?
- What are some of reasons that distortion occurs?
- How does this activity relate to the communication process in general?
- What can be done to improve communication?

Electricity

Objective

To pass a pulse (hand squeeze) around the group circle.

Time Required

Five minutes.

Group Size

Five to twenty-five participants.

Materials

None.

Preparation

None.

Process

1. Instruct the participants to form a large circle, with participants holding hands. Join the circle as one of the players.

2. Announce that it is time for the group to get a shot of energy. Explain that the energy will be in the form of an "electrical current" that will move around the circle by means of a hand squeeze passing from person to person. The current will first pass around one way, then the other.

3. Start the "current" by squeezing the hand of one of the participants next to you. After the pulse (hand squeeze) returns to you, send it in the other direction.

4. Once the pulse returns to you again, squeeze the hands of both persons next to you. That means two energy pulses are going in opposite directions. One person will receive energy from both directions at once and will have to squeeze back with both hands to keep the two energy pulses going.

5. After managing this, direct the players to close their eyes. Begin by passing a single pulse (hand squeeze), then send two more energy pulses. Continue to add new energy pulses in less and less time, until you begin to hear laughter. Bring the activity to an end.

Discussion

- How did you feel as the pulses came more and more frequently?
- How can we relate what happened in this activity to the workplace?

End Game

Objective

To complete a letter puzzle that reveals a closing message.

Group Size

An unlimited number of participants.

Time Required

Five minutes.

Materials

One copy of the End Game Worksheet and a pencil for each participant.

Preparation

None.

Process

1. Distribute a pencil and one copy of the End Game Worksheet face down to each participant.

2. Explain that participants are to use the series of clues on the worksheet to make the appropriate entry into each block of the puzzle. The first person to complete the puzzle is to stand immediately and announce the solution aloud.

3. Direct the participants to turn over the worksheets and begin. The activity stops when the first person announces the puzzle's solution.

Solution

"TIME IS UP"

Discussion

- Did you answer the questions in order or randomly?
- Did the pressure to be the first to finish affect your performance in any way? Why or why not?
- How does this relate to problem solving in general?

End Game Worksheet

Directions: Using the clues given below, fill in each block with the appropriate entry.

1. If more than half of the months of the year have an R in their names, place an I in spaces 2 and 6; otherwise, use an O.

2. If there are 120 pencils in a gross, place an H in space 7, unless there are 144, in which case use an S.

3. If Pat and Pamela are girls' names, put an S in space 1, unless Pat is sometimes a boy's name, in which case do nothing.

4. If the River Seine is in Italy, put an E in space 8, unless Perth is an Australian city, in which case put a E in space 4.

5. If the North Star is the brightest star in the sky, place an S in space 5; otherwise, darken the space.

6. If a collie is a dog, put a U in space 9, unless carrots are sold by the ear, in which case put an L in space 9.

7. Put an M in space 1, unless rhubarb is edible, in which case put it in space 3.

8. If Ernest Hemingway wrote "Islands in the Stream," put a T in space 1. If Joseph Conrad wrote "Lord Jim," put a T in space 10 also.

9. If 9 and 8 are 16, put an S in space 4. If they are not 16, put a T in space 10, unless Cinderella went to the ball, in which case darken space 8.

10. If Jack Horner pulled a prune out of his pie, put a K in space 10. If it was a peach, put an N in space 10; but if it was a plum, put a P in space 10.

Guiding Light

Objective

To lead a partner through a series of movements nonverbally.

Time Required

Five to ten minutes.

Group Size

An unlimited number of participants, who will work in pairs.

Materials

Stopwatch or clock with second hand.

Preparation

None.

Process

1. Instruct the participants to form pairs, then designate one partner as A and the other as B. Partners A and B are to stand facing one another, with the outside tips of their right shoes almost touching, toes pointing in opposite directions. The left foot should be placed slightly behind the right one in a comfortable, balanced position. Demonstrate the stance with a participant as shown below.

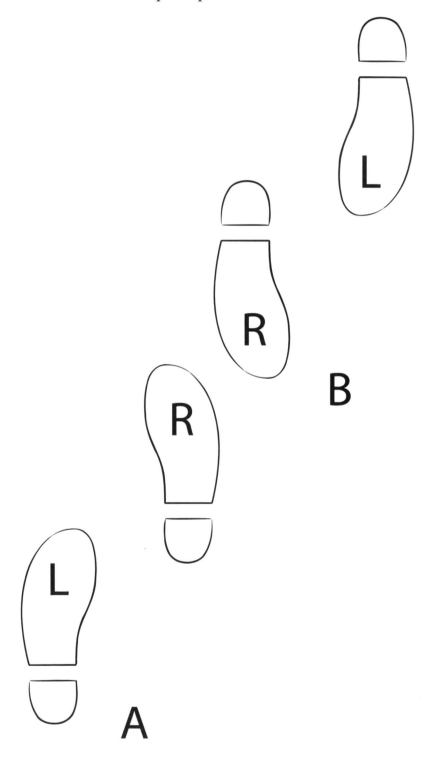

2. Announce that Partner A will be the leader and Partner B will be the follower in the first round.

3. Direct the partners to raise their right arms, palms facing, and touch wrists. Explain that the leader will move his or her right arm, and/or whole body, in light, rhythmic, and flowing motions. The goal is to lead nonverbally so that the partner follows with ease and grace, almost as in a dance.

4. Signal for the activity to begin and time for thirty to sixty seconds, then stop the participants.

5. Tell the pairs to reverse roles and repeat the procedure for the second round. Signal for the activity to begin and time it for thirty to sixty seconds, then stop the participants.

6. Repeat the process with new partners, as time allows.

Discussion

- How difficult was it to follow the leader's movements?
- Did the exercise become easier with practice? Why or why not?
- How does this exercise relate to the principle, "Lead by example"?

In Gear

Objective

To mesh individual groups into one operating machine.

Time Required

Ten to fifteen minutes.

Group Size

Fifteen to thirty-five participants, who will work in three or more groups of variable sizes. (*NOTE:* Each successive group is to contain two or three additional members.)

Materials

Clock or stopwatch.

Preparation

Based on the number of participants, calculate how many groups will be utilized. Next determine the number of members needed for each group, with the size of successive groups building by two or three each.

Process

1. Instruct the participants to form three (or more) groups of the predetermined number of participants. (For example, a group of twenty-two participants could be divided into three groups of five, seven, and ten members, respectively.)

2. Explain that each group will become a "gear" by forming a *tight* circle facing inward with members grasping one another's hands.

3. Direct the "gears" (groups) to gather together in the center of the room. Have the groups form circles next to each other in ascending order of size.

4. Announce that the purpose of the activity is for the smallest gear to "mesh" with the next largest one, which then meshes with the next largest one, and so on, until all form into one operating machine. Explain that each player is a "gear tooth." As the gears turn, the members of one group circle are to "mesh," that is, fit into the spaces between the gear teeth of the adjoining circle. Explain that the smallest gear is the controlling one; it can speed up or slow down, causing the other gears to follow suit.

5. Begin the action by telling the smallest gear to begin turning, which will start the other gears turning. Allow several minutes to pass before stopping the groups.

Variation

You can add to the fun by reversing the direction by saying "Change!" during the course of action. Announce to participants that they are to make a screeching sound as they put on the brakes and go into reverse whenever they hear the direction to change.

Discussion

- How did you feel about the smallest gear controlling the action?
- Was the activity difficult to perform? Why or why not?
- How does this activity relate to the concept of leadership?
- How does this activity relate to teamwork in general?
- Why is it important for all groups within an organization to work well with one another?

Keeping Things Afloat

Objective

To work together as a group to keep weighted balloons in the air.

Time Required

Five to ten minutes.

Group Size

Six to twenty participants, who will work in groups of six to ten.

Materials

One round, non-latex balloon and one marble for each participant, plus one additional balloon and marble per group; clock or timer.

Preparation

Insert a marble into each balloon, then inflate and tie off the ends. (*NOTE:* You will need a large open area for this activity.)

Process

1. Instruct participants to form groups of approximately six to ten members each. Place each group in a separate location, allowing sufficient space for movement.

2. Distribute one prepared balloon to each participant. Provide one member from each group with an extra balloon.

3. Explain that the goal is for each group to keep all its balloons in the air at the same time for a period of two minutes. Group members are to wait for the signal before they hit their balloons into the air.

4. Signal for the activity to begin, timing the activity for two minutes. Stop the activity when time expires.

Variation

Mix the composition of the balloons for each group, providing some weighted by the marbles and some without the marbles.

Discussion

- How difficult was it to keep all the balloons in the air? Why? *(The marble in each balloon makes it bounce in all kinds of directions.)*

- How well did your group's members work together? Why?

- In what way(s) does this activity relate to teamwork in general?

Keyboard

Objective

To simulate the typing of individual letters in a predetermined sentence.

Time Required

Five minutes.

Group Size

Twenty to thirty participants.

Materials

Flip chart and felt-tipped marker.

Preparation

Create a sentence that uses all of the letters of the alphabet, for example, "The quick brown fox jumps over the lazy dog." Write the sentence on the flip chart.

Process

1. Instruct all participants to gather into a circle. Assign one letter of the alphabet (A through Z) to each player. If there are fewer players than letters, assign more than one letter to some participants. If there are more players than letters, others can become periods, commas, spaces, or an eraser for correcting mistakes.

2. Create a typewriter rhythm for everyone to follow. For example, the appropriate player claps hands, stamps a foot once, or punches the key by raising a hand in the air.

3. Referring to the sentence on the prepared flip chart, explain that the object of the game is to type out the entire sentence using the proper keys. For example, when the signal is given to begin, the person with the first letter of the sentence makes the prescribed motion and calls out the appropriate letter. Then, the player with the next letter makes the motion and calls out his or her letter. When a space is reached, everyone calls out the word "Space" in unison. If a mistake is made, participants are to keep going, unless there is a person designated as the eraser to call out "Correction."

4. Signal for the activity to begin and continue until the motions for the designated sentence are completed.

Discussion

- How difficult was it to coordinate the appropriate sequences for this activity?
- How does this relate to coordination of efforts in the workplace?

Match Mates

Objective

To locate the duplicates of assigned articles.

Time Required

Five to ten minutes.

Group Size

Ten to forty participants, who will work in groups of three or four.

Materials

One envelope for each group; duplicate pairs of a variety of small articles (such as rubber bands, safety pins, paper clips, screws, corks, pins, nails, beads, buttons, washers, coins, or beans), plus several additional items that are of the same category but are not exact duplicates; group prizes; clock or timer. (*NOTE:* It is possible to have more than one pair of the same article by marking them differently. For instance, one pair of pins could be used as is, one pair with paint or nail polish on the heads, and one pair with the ends bent.)

Preparation

Prior to the session, conceal over as wide an area as possible a variety of small articles, one from each of the duplicate pairs, as well as "same-category" additional items. Prepare one envelope for each participating group by placing in each approximately six articles that are duplicates of the hidden ones.

Process

1. Instruct the participants to form groups of three or four members each.

2. Distribute one prepared envelope to each group.

3. Explain that the groups are to find the article corresponding to each one they have in the envelope. Emphasize that the identical match must be found. For instance, if an aspirin has a cross inked on it, another with a cross is required to complete the pair. Announce that any group locating a match for all of its items will win a prize.

4. Signal for the activity to begin, timing it for approximately five minutes before telling the groups to stop.

5. Determine how many pairs each group was able to locate. Present a prize to any group that has located the duplicate of all the items in its envelope.

Discussion

- How well did members of your group coordinate their efforts?

- Were other groups willing to negotiate in order to obtain duplicate items? Why or why not?

- How can we relate this activity to cross-functional teams? To teamwork in general?

Meet You at the Pass

Objective

To pass two balls simultaneously so that one catches up with the other.

Time Required

Five to ten minutes.

Group Size

Ten to thirty participants.

Materials

Two beach balls or large play balls; clock or timer.

Preparation

If using beach balls, inflate both.

Process

1. Instruct the participants to form a large circle.

2. Distribute one ball each to two individuals on opposite sides of the circle.

3. Explain that, on your signal, each ball is to be passed to the right. The balls are to be *handed* around the circle as fast as possible. The object is for one ball to try to catch up to the other.

4. Signal for the game to begin. (*NOTE:* To add a new component of difficulty, you may call "Reverse" from time to time so that the balls change direction.)

5. Stop the activity when one ball catches up to the other, or after approximately five minutes.

Discussion

- How did you feel during the activity?
- How did this game rely on cooperation?
- Did elements of competition develop during the game? Why or why not?
- How can we relate this activity to situations in the workplace?

Mind Over Matter

Objective

To answer riddles that require thoughtful reasoning.

Time Required

Ten minutes.

Group Size

An unlimited number of participants.

Materials

One copy of the Mind Over Matter Worksheet and a pencil for each participant; clock or stopwatch.

Preparation

None.

Process

1. Explain that participants will receive a sheet containing questions that they are to read and answer as quickly as possible. They will have exactly two minutes to complete the "test." Tell the participants that they are to keep the sheets face down until instructed to begin.

2. Distribute a pencil and one copy of the Mind Over Matter Worksheet, face down, to each participant.

3. Signal for the participants to begin the test. Time for two minutes, then stop the activity.

4. Review each question, in turn. First, obtain feedback from the participants; then reveal the correct answers, as given below.

Solution

1. None; all in the directory are listed.
2. Schubert wrote the "Unfinished Symphony."
3. Mount Everest; it existed, although it was not yet discovered.
4. Neither; the plane was over the Gulf of Mexico, so they both hit the water.
5. One large haystack.
6. The window.
7. He drove in reverse.
8. She put the sugar into a can of ground coffee.
9. The word "incorrectly."
10. In total darkness, none of them could see a thing.

Discussion

- How well did you do on the "test"?
- What was your reaction when you heard the correct answer to each question?
- How did a tendency to jump to conclusions affect how you answered the questions?
- Why is it important to examine information closely during the problem-solving process?

Mind Over Matter Worksheet

Directions: These questions are designed to test your wits. Write down the answer as soon as possible after reading each question. You have two minutes to complete the worksheet.

1. In Camberwell, Australia, two out of every seven people have telephone numbers that are not listed in the directory. If there are 14,000 names in the Camberwell telephone directory, how many of them have numbers that are unlisted?

2. Why is it that Beethoven never finished the "Unfinished Symphony"?

3. What was the highest mountain in the world before Mount Everest was discovered?

4. A mail plane was halfway from Dallas, Texas, to Miami, Florida, at a height of 2,400 feet on a clear, still day. It dropped a 100-kg sack of letters and a 100-kg steel rod at the same time. Which hit the ground first?

5. A farmer had four haystacks in one field and twice as many in each of his other two fields. If he put the haystacks from all three fields together, how many would he have?

6. What is the invention, first discovered in ancient times, that allows people to see through solid walls?

7. A man carefully pointed his car due east and then drove for two miles. He was then two miles west of where he started from. Why?

8. A woman unwrapped a lump of sugar and put it into her coffee, but the sugar did not get wet. Why?

9. What common word is pronounced incorrectly by a majority of Yale and Harvard graduates?

10. Which animal would see best in total darkness: an owl, a leopard, or an eagle?

Modified Objects

Objective

To describe objects using only adjectives.

Time Required

Five minutes.

Group Size

Six to thirty participants, who will work in groups of three.

Materials

One sheet of paper and a pencil for each participant; clock with second hand or stopwatch.

Preparation

None.

Process

1. Instruct the participants to form groups of three members each. Within each group, one person is to be designated the sender.

2. Distribute one sheet of paper and a pencil to each participant.

3. Direct the sender in each group to think about an object he or she possesses and to write the name of that object secretly on the sheet of paper, keeping it concealed from other members of the group. Explain that the sender will have thirty seconds to use a series of one-word adjectives to describe the object to the other two members. After each word is given, the receiving members will write their guesses sequentially on their individual sheets of paper. At the end of the round, the two players will make their final guesses and the sender will reveal the object described.

4. Direct the senders to begin their descriptions, and time the group for thirty seconds. Stop the activity when time expires.

5. Direct the other members of the group to make their guesses; then have the senders reveal the object.

6. Repeat the procedure described in Steps 3 through 5 until all three group members have had an opportunity to present a description.

Discussion

- How accurate were the guesses made by the receiving players?
- How did successive descriptors affect your guesses?
- Why is clear and concise communication important?

On-Line

Objective

To have each participant follow the movements of the person directly in front of him or her.

Time Required

Ten minutes.

Group Size

Twenty to forty participants, who will work in two and then four teams.

Materials

None.

Preparation

None.

Process

1. Instruct the participants to gather into two equal-sized groups, each forming a single line. The first person in each line will be designated the leader. The lines should be placed so that the two leaders face each other, as shown below.

X X X X **X**   **X** X X X X
                Leader A   Leader B

2. Explain that the object of the game is to follow the movements of the person directly in front of you, rather than following the leader directly. Each leader will begin a motion that is to be passed down the line. For example, if the leader raises his or her left arm, the second person follows the leader, then the third follows the second person, and so on until the movement reaches the last person. The leader should remain in place while performing each action, moving arms and legs, bending, leaning, jumping, reaching, and so forth. This process of the leader introducing successive new movements should continue, without pause, until you indicate that it is time to stop.

3. Signal for each leader to begin his or her actions. After the players have performed a series of several movements, stop the activity.

4. Direct the leader of each group to exchange places with the last person in line, who will become the new leader. Designate one group as "A" and the other as "B." For the next series of movements, the process will remain the same, but the leader of group "B" is to mirror the movements of the leader of group "A."

5. Signal for the leader of group "A" to begin his or her actions. After several moves, indicate that the leaders are to switch roles. After several more movements, stop the activity.

6. Finally, divide the group into four teams, facing each other in an X formation as shown below. The first person in each group will be designated group leader.

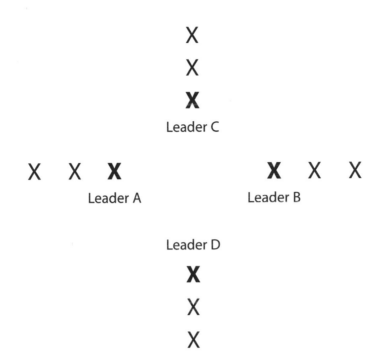

7. Explain that Leaders A and C will initiate their own separate moves. Leader B will follow the movements of Leader A and Leader D will follow those of Leader C. As each leader starts a movement, the second group member sends on the motion, with each successive group member repeating the movement of the person in front of him or her until it once again is passed down the entire line.

8. Signal for Leaders A and C to begin their actions. After several more movements, stop the activity.

Discussion

- In general, how difficult was this task? Why?
- Which group formation made it most difficult to perform? Why?
- How did the leaders feel about their roles?
- How can we relate this activity to the concept of leadership? To teamwork?

Pandemonium

Objective

To follow directions in direct conflict with those given to others.

Time Required

Five minutes.

Group Size

Six to eighteen participants, who will work in groups of six.

Materials

Two sheets of paper, one small box or bag, and a newspaper section for each group; scissors; felt-tipped pen; small box or bag.

Preparation

For each team:

(1) Cut each of two 8½" x 11" sheets of paper into thirds.

(2) Write the following message on three of the slips of paper then fold them in half:

"You must do all in your power to keep the newspaper
neatly folded on the floor."

(3) Write the following message on three of the slips of paper, then fold them in half:

"You must tear the newspaper apart
and toss the pieces into the air."

(4) Place each set of six folded slips into a small box or bag.

Process

1. Instruct the participants to form groups of six members each, located in separate areas. Have each group form a circle.
2. Distribute a box (or bag) of prepared instruction slips to one member of each group.
3. Tell each group member to pick one folded sheet of instructions out of the group's box or bag and to wait until you signal for them to read the instructions.
4. Place a folded newspaper section on the floor in the center of each group, then signal for participants to read their slips of paper and to begin acting on the instructions.
5. Observe how each group behaves, as half the members of each group have conflicting instructions from the other half. Stop the activity after a few minutes.

Discussion

- How did you feel about following your instructions while others were trying to do the opposite?
- Do individuals sometimes have conflicting goals? Why?
- How do organizational and personal goals sometimes conflict?
- How can we relate this activity to what happens in the workplace?

Pass Out

Objective

To pass cards around a circle until a winning hand is completed.

Time Required

Five to ten minutes.

Group Size

Eight to thirteen participants. (*NOTE:* The variation can accommodate an unlimited number of participants, who will work in groups of four to seven.)

Materials

One deck of playing cards. (*Variation:* one deck of playing cards for each group.)

Preparation

None.

Process

1. Gather the participants into a circle. Deal four playing cards to each person.

2. Explain that the object of the game is for each participant to receive four matching cards, one in each suit, in his or her own hand. This is to be accomplished by each person passing an unwanted card face down to the player on his or her immediate left. This process continues until a player obtains four matching cards to "win." A player is to raise his or her hand to indicate a win.

3. Signal for the play to begin. Stop the activity when someone has four matching cards.

Variation

Play in groups of four to seven participants, with one deck of playing cards for each team. Deal seven cards to each person. Cards are passed one a time to the left and play continues until someone obtains all cards in the same suit.

Discussion

- What was your playing strategy?
- Did this strategy change throughout the game? Why?
- How does this relate to how you or others might behave in the real world?

Passing the Buck

Objective

To pass along an object to trigger storytelling.

Time Required

Ten to fifteen minutes.

Group Size

Five to twenty participants.

Materials

Tossable object (for example, a beanbag or small foam ball); clock or timer.

Preparation

None.

Process

1. Instruct the participants to stand in a circle.

2. Explain that participants will be passing the "buck" (any small object that can be tossed easily from one player to another without harm) from one player to another. The first person receiving the object must begin to tell a story—made up on the spot. This player will then toss the "buck" to another person, who must catch it and continue the story. The story can take any form, just as long as there is an attempt to connect it to the last player's contribution. Emphasize that players must not break the flow of the story no matter how fast the object is passed. Those who catch the object must speak—if only a few words—and then they can toss the object to another person. Participants will continue to pass the object until time is called.

3. Give the tossable object to one participant and ask him or her to begin the story. Allow approximately five minutes for the activity to continue, then call time.

4. If time allows, repeat Step 3 for another round.

Variation

As a review session for content matter, have the participants discuss something related to the specific topic as they receive the "buck."

Discussion

- How did you feel when the "buck" was passed to you? Why?
- How hard was it to conduct a coherent narrative?
- What factors contributed to the difficulty of the task?
- How does this activity relate to situations in the workplace?

Playing Taps

Objective

To relax and refresh through light tapping and slapping.

Time Required

Ten minutes.

Group Size

An unlimited number of participants, who will work in groups of three.

Materials

Clock or timer.

Preparation

None.

Process

1. Explain that this activity is designed to refresh tired minds and bodies through light tapping and slapping, which are supposed to generate alpha waves, producing a state of relaxed concentration. Participation is voluntary; individuals who choose not to participate in the process may wish to perform some other action that is personally relaxing, for example, stretching, closing eyes, or "shaking out" arms and legs.

2. Describe the process as follows. Within each group, one person is to bend forward at the waist, letting his or her arms hang loosely down in front. Another group member will *lightly* tap with fingertips around the back of the person's head, neck, and shoulders while the third group member very *gently* slaps the person's back and arms with a quick, continuing motion. The effect of the tapping should be like pattering drops of rain, and the slapping should be like lapping waves.

3. Instruct all those who are participating to form groups of three members each. Tell group members to assign roles as tapper, slapper, and recipient.

4. Signal for the groups to begin. Time for approximately one minute, then tell the members to change roles. After an additional minute, have members change roles once more. Time the final minute, then stop the activity.

Discussion

- How did you feel during the exercise? Why?
- How does stress affect your ability to work effectively?
- What are some other things you can do to become relaxed and refreshed?

Quick Takes

Objective

To use a simple and rapid means of obtaining individual reactions to various issues.

Time Required

Five to fifteen minutes.

Group Size

Eight to thirty participants.

Materials

Prepared question(s).

Preparation

Depending on the amount of time available, prepare one or more questions to be asked of the participants that relate to issues pertinent to the training, or these may be of a more general nature, such as:

- What is something you are proud of?
- What is one thing about which you have changed your mind recently?

- How did you handle a recent disagreement?
- What is one thing you would change in your organization?
- What is one thing you would change in your work life?
- What is one thing you would change in your personal life?

Process

1. Explain to the participants that you will be asking a question to which they will respond. Their answers should be brief and to the point, although a participant may give a little background to explain his or her answer, if necessary. Any participant may choose to pass.

2. Pose the question to the group and provide a few moments for the participants to think about their answers. Quickly "whip" around the room, calling on participants to give their answers. Do not allow participants to spend too much time on individual answers.

3. Facilitate a group discussion using the questions presented below.

4. Repeat Steps 2 and 3 for a new question, as time allows. Repeat if desired.

Discussion

- How did you feel about revealing your thoughts in this manner?
- What insights did you gain on the topic?

Revolution

Objective

To complete circuits around obstacles as an intact group.

Time Required

Five to ten minutes.

Group Size

Fifteen to forty participants.

Materials

Four large boxes; flip chart and felt-tipped marker; stopwatch or clock with second hand.

Preparation

A large open space is required.

Process

1. Instruct the participants to hold hands and form a large circle. Designate one person as the leader.

2. Referring to the diagram below, place two of the boxes inside the circle at opposite ends. The other two boxes are to be placed outside the circle approximately midway from the boxes located inside. The group will be moving around the boxes in a modified figure-eight pattern.

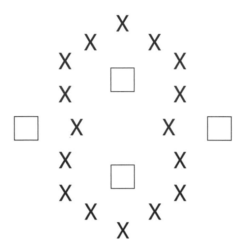

3. Explain that the task is for the group to move one complete revolution clockwise, then one complete revolution counterclockwise without touching the boxes or letting go of their partners' hands. This is to be done in the shortest time possible.

4. Signal for the activity to begin, noting the time it takes for the group leader to return to the original position after completing both revolutions. Stop the activity when the revolutions have been completed and record the time on the flip chart.

5. Repeat the process for two more tries, each time encouraging the group to try to better its previous times.

Discussion

- How difficult was it to perform the task? Why?
- What impact did the boxes have as obstacles to the group's performance?
- How can we relate this activity to situations in the workplace?

Ring Around the String

Objective

To discover the player secretly holding the ring.

Time Required

Five to ten minutes.

Group Size

Eight to twenty participants.

Materials

Heavy string long enough to reach around the circle of players; one small ring (a metal washer works well); clock or timer.

Preparation

Thread the long piece of string through the ring and tightly tie the ends of the string together. The ring should slide along the string easily.

Process

1. Direct the participants to sit or stand in a circle, facing in. Select one person to be the contestant, who will stand in the middle of the circle.

2. Give the prepared string to the remaining participants to hold. Each person should hold the string with both hands so that it makes a loose circle inside the group.

3. Explain that the object of the game is for the players to pass the ring along the string, from one fist to another, without revealing who has it. The contestant in the middle is to watch the others carefully. The players are to slide their hands back and forth over the string, even when they are not passing the ring, so that the contestant cannot be sure where the ring actually is. When the contestant guesses correctly, he or she then joins the circle, and the one who was caught with the ring becomes the new contestant.

4. Signal for the activity to begin. Observe the process for approximately five minutes, then stop the activity.

Discussion

- For the contestants, what observations did you make to determine who was holding the ring?
- Were players able to work together to conceal the ring from the contestant? Why or why not?
- Are some things kept concealed in the workplace? What is the effect of this?

Robotics

Objective

To guide human robots.

Time Required

Five to ten minutes.

Group Size

Twelve to fifty participants, who will work in groups of three or four.

Materials

Stopwatch or clock.

Preparation

None.

Process

1. Instruct the participants to form groups of three or four members each. Have each group select one person to be the leader.

2. Explain that, with the exception of the leader, all members of a group are to act as robots. Upon the signal, the group leader will start up the robots and guide them during the activity. The robots may only go in a straight line until their direction is changed by the leader. If a robot runs into an obstacle or another robot, it must send out a beeping signal (that is, the robot says, "Beep-beep-beep") until it is redirected by the leader. The object is to keep the robots functional at all times.

3. Signal for the activity to begin. Time for one to two minutes, then stop the groups.

4. Direct the groups to get together and choose new leaders and repeat the action.

5. Signal for the new activity to begin. Time for approximately two minutes, then stop the action. Repeat, with new leaders, if desired.

Discussion

- How did the leaders (guides) feel during the activity?
- What conditions influenced the leaders' effectiveness?
- How does this relate to the leader's role in the workplace?

Rules and Regulations

Objective

To determine rules that provide structure.

Time Required

Five to fifteen minutes.

Group Size

Five to twenty participants.

Materials

None.

Preparation

None.

Process

1. Explain that rules give structure to games, but that most rules are unspoken and invisible. In this exercise, participants will have a chance to design some rules to see how the process works.

2. Instruct the participants to sit or stand in a circle, then select one person to leave the room.

3. Have the remaining players choose a rule that will be followed in the course of answering questions about themselves. The questions will be posed by the absent participant when he or she returns in an attempt to determine the rule that has been set. Provide the following rules as examples:

   • Answer questions as if you were the person to the right.

   • Nod your head after answering the question.

   • Answer questions in the completely opposite way.

4. Allow a few minutes for the group to discuss and choose the rule that will be followed. Have the group verbally state the rule so that all participants are aware of it.

5. Have the absent participant reenter the room. Explain that he or she must determine the rule the group has set by asking the other players questions about themselves. The person trying to guess the rule is allowed to take as long as needed.

6. Repeat the procedure as time allows.

Variations

1. Choose a group of two or three participants as "guessers" who will leave the room together, then return and alternate asking questions. At the end of each round of questions, they will discuss what they think the rule(s) are before continuing the questioning. The exercise ends when group members agree to make their final guess.

2. To make the exercise a little more difficult, have the group impose more than one rule.

Discussion

• For the guessing player, what process did you use to help determine the set rule?

• How do rules, formal and informal, affect work situations?

• What impact does the culture of the organization (that is, norms and expectations) have on work situations?

Scout Out

Objective

To attempt to reach specific individual places while holding hands as a group.

Time Required

Five minutes.

Group Size

Ten to thirty participants.

Materials

None.

Preparation

None.

Process

1. Instruct the participants to form a large circle, holding hands.

2. Tell the participants that each one of them is to "scout out" a particular secret spot in the room where he or she would like to be. Give the participants a moment to choose their spots.

3. Tell the participants that they now should try to reach their secret spots without letting go of one another's hands.

4. Allow the participants one to two minutes to attempt this challenge, then stop the activity.

Discussion

- How many of you reached your secret spot?
- What factors influenced your ability to do so?
- How does this activity relate to the topic of personal needs versus group responsibilities?
- How does this relate to situations in the workplace?

Square Off

Objective

To maintain a prescribed square formation in relation to the leader.

Time Required

Five to ten minutes.

Group Size

Twelve to twenty-four participants.

Materials

None.

Preparation

None.

Process

1. Instruct the participants to form a square with an approximately equal number of people on each of the four sides. When everyone is in position, stand in the middle of the square and announce that you will be the leader.

2. Explain that the object of the game is for the participants on all four sides of the square to remain in the same position in relation to you, in the middle. This means that those in front stay in front of you, while people in back stay in back of you, those on the right stay on the right, and participants on the left must stay on the left. Whenever you move into a new position, the people comprising the square must move themselves into the same position as before as quickly as possible.

3. Before you begin, make sure that everyone knows his or her position. Then, quickly face in a different direction and say, "Square off." See how quickly everyone moves to reestablish the square around you. You may turn a little or a lot—one time a 30-degree turn and the next time a 180-degree turn, for example. Continue to make several quick turns, then call time.

Discussion

- Was it difficult for the group as a whole to maintain the square formation? Why or why not?

- How well did individuals adjust to the changes that occurred?

- What impact does leadership have on individual performance? Group performance?

- In what ways can we relate this activity to the workplace?

Symphony of Syllables

Objective

To discern a word by hearing the separate syllables sung at the same time.

Time Required

Ten to fifteen minutes.

Group Size

An unlimited number of participants.

Materials

None.

Preparation

None.

Process

1. Instruct the participants to form a large circle. Select one person to leave the room.

2. Explain that the rest of the group will pick one word with three or more syllables, such as the word "Sep-tem-ber." Tell them to select the word and count the number of syllables.

3. Direct the participants to count off by the number of syllables; for example, if the word has three syllables, the participants would count off as 1, 2, and 3, until all have been assigned a number. Those with 1 would be the first syllable ("sep"), those with 2 become the second syllable ("tem"), and those with 3 are the third syllable ("ber").

4. Have the group pick a song with a simple melody such as "Row, Row, Row Your Boat" or "Yankee Doodle." Explain that each person is to sing the assigned syllable over and over to the tune of the chosen song. For example, 1s would sing "sep, sep, sep," 2s would sing "tem, tem, tem," and 3s would sing "ber, ber, ber" at the same time to the same melody.

5. Call the person who left the room to return. He or she must listen carefully as the group is singing and try to piece together the word. One minute is allowed in which to guess the word.

6. If desired, select another person to leave the room and repeat the process.

Discussion

- How difficult was it to guess the word? Why?
- What similar influences on the communication process occur in the workplace?

Talk Fest

Objective

To have partners carry on simultaneous conversations.

Time Required

Five to ten minutes.

Group Size

Four to thirty participants, who will work in pairs.

Materials

Clock with a second hand or a stopwatch.

Preparation

None.

Process

1. Instruct the participants to divide into two equal groups and to line up in two rows.

2. Direct those participants in one row to stand back to back with those in the other row. Announce that the players standing back to back will be partners.

3. Explain that when you give the signal, the players are to turn around quickly and face their partners. They must talk to one another without stopping. They must both talk at the same time, about anything at all, and what they say does not have to make sense. All players must keep this up for one minute.

4. Give a signal to begin the activity. Time the activity for one minute, then tell the participants to stop.

Discussion

- How did you feel during the activity?
- Was it difficult to continue talking for the full minute? Why or why not?
- Were you able to distinguish what your partner was saying? Why or why not?
- How does this relate to communication in the workplace?

Tally Up

Objective

To create an ongoing list of information within an assigned category.

Time Required

Ongoing. Best used for training that meets in several sessions over an extended period of time.

Group Size

An unlimited number of participants.

Materials

Roll of brown wrapping paper or several sheets of newsprint paper; felt-tipped marker; tape or tacks.

Preparation

Choose an empty wall and tape or tack up a large piece of wrapping paper or several newsprint sheets. Place in an area that is accessible to all participants and where it can remain all the time. Select a category, preferably something that will allow for inventive interpretations, and write the category chosen across the top of the paper. Suggested categories include: things that are associated with the number 3; little-known statistics or trivia; things that are yellow; things you wish for; favorite personal possessions.

Process

1. Referring to the posted paper, explain that participants are encouraged to create a list of items relating to the category written on the sheet. Items may be added to the list during breaks and at any other free time throughout the session.

2. For a workshop that runs over an extended period, replace the sheets with new categories from time to time. Save the sheets that have been taken down for review at the end of the last session.

3. At the end of the last session, review some of the information that was listed for each category.

Discussion

- Did you learn anything about the group as a whole through the information that was listed? What did you learn?

- What were some of the more creative additions to the list(s)?

- How do organizations support creativity? Hinder creativity?

Thumbs Up

Objective

To keep all participants actively involved in a discussion.

Time Required

Five to fifteen minutes.

Group Size

Six to thirty participants, who will work in groups of six to ten.

Materials

List of discussion topics; clock or timer.

Preparation

Determine specific topics for group discussion.

Process

1. Instruct the participants to form groups of six to ten members each, seated in circles.

2. Explain that participants will be asked to discuss a particular topic within their groups. To keep all participants actively involved in the discussion, each person is to extend his or her fist toward the middle of the circle. Once the discussion begins, each member is to share, in any order, *one* piece of information on the topic. As each person shares, his or her thumb will go up. A person may not share again until all thumbs have been turned up. When all the thumbs are up, members begin again and continue the process, giving equal opportunity for input.

3. Announce the topic for discussion and signal for the groups to begin. Allow approximately five minutes, then stop the discussion.

4. Tell the participants that the process will be followed once again, but with a new discussion topic. Announce the new topic and signal for the groups to begin. Allow approximately five minutes, then stop the activity.

Discussion

- How did you feel about this process? Why?
- Did you become more comfortable with the process as time progressed? Why or why not?
- How can this process, or one similar to it, be utilized in the workplace?

Transformations

Objective

To form into human representations of designated objects.

Time Required

Ten to fifteen minutes.

Group Size

Ten to twenty-five participants, who will work in groups of five to eight.

Materials

Clock or stopwatch.

Preparation

None.

Process

1. Instruct the participants to form groups of five to eight members each.

2. Explain that the object is for group members to form into human representations of whatever object is announced, *within a two-minute time limit.* For example, if the object announced is a helicopter, group members must link together into items such as propellers, a cockpit, and landing gears.

3. Call out the name of an object. Suggestions include such items as a ship, tree, cathedral, waterfall, truck, bus, skyscraper, or suspension bridge. Time the groups for two minutes while they arrange themselves into that shape. Give a thirty-second warning before time expires, then call time.

4. Repeat the process with other designated objects, as time allows.

Discussion

- How well did members of your group work together?
- What factors influenced your group's performance?
- In what ways do groups need to adjust to change?

Visionaries

Objective

To become focused on the environment and its effect on perception.

Time Required

Five minutes.

Group Size

An unlimited number of participants.

Materials

One sheet of paper and a pencil for each participant.

Preparation

None.

Process

1. Distribute one sheet of paper and a pencil to each participant.

2. Ask the participants to look around the room and notice three things that they have not noticed previously. Each person is to write the items he or she noticed on the sheet of paper.

3. Have participants read items from their lists, asking others to raise their hands if they have the same item.

Variation

Have participants look around the room and make note of three things that they perceive to symbolize the organization or some aspect of the topic of the workshop (for example, communication, conflict, problem solving, and so on).

Discussion

- Why do people have a tendency to take a situation for granted?
- How does this apply to situations in the workplace?

Variation Discussion

- Why do people perceive things in different ways?
- How does this impact situations in the workplace?

Group
Challenges

Alpha-Bits

Objective

To form words that begin and end with the same letter of the alphabet.

Time Required

Ten minutes.

Group Size

An unlimited number of participants, who will work in groups of three or four.

Materials

One copy of the Alpha-Bits Worksheet and a pencil for each participant; clock or timer.

Preparation

None.

Process

1. Instruct the participants to form groups of three or four members each.

2. Distribute one copy of the Alpha-Bits Worksheet and a pencil to each participant.

3. Explain that each group will have five minutes to list as many words as possible that start and end with the same letter. They will do this for each letter of the alphabet, with the exception of Q. Groups should attempt to find the longest possible word for each letter, because they will score one point for each letter of each word listed. The highest total score wins.

    Give the following example of two words that earn a total of eleven points:

    A AMNESIA = 7 points

    B BARB = 4 points

4. Signal for the activity to begin. Time the group work for five minutes, then call time.

5. Tell groups to calculate their total points. Allow several minutes for the process to occur. Determine the group with the highest number of total points.

Discussion

- How well did group members work together on this activity?
- What, if anything, made the activity difficult to do? Why or why not?
- How can we relate this activity to the use of available resources in the workplace?

Alpha-Bits Worksheet

Letter	Word	Points
A		
B		
C		
D		
E		
F		
G		
H		
I		
J		
K		
L		
M		
N		
O		
P		
R		
S		
T		
U		
V		
W		
X		
Y		
Z		

TOTAL:

Boggled

Objective

To form words by compiling connected letters.

Time Required

Ten minutes.

Group Size

An unlimited number of participants, who will work in groups of three.

Materials

One copy of the Boggled Worksheet and a pencil for each group; flip chart and felt-tipped marker; clock or timer.

Preparation

None.

Process

1. Instruct the participants to form groups of three members each.

2. Distribute one copy of the Boggled Worksheet and a pencil to each group.

3. Explain that this activity is based on the popular cube game Boggle®. The goal is for each group to score as many points as possible in a three-minute time period. Referring to the top of the worksheet, read aloud the following information:

   Rules: Each group member in turn contributes a word. To count, one letter in a word must be connected to a previous letter by a side or a corner and no letter may be "doubled." For example, at the top right, "TON" is an acceptable word, but "TOO" is not. However, once you pass from one letter to another, you may return to any previously used letter. For example, at the bottom left, "WOW" is an acceptable word.

   Scoring: Each word is worth the square of the number of letters it contains. A two-letter word is worth four points (2 x 2) but a four-letter word is worth sixteen points (4 x 4).

4. Signal for the group work to begin, then time the activity for three minutes. Stop the groups when time expires.

5. Allow several minutes for groups to calculate their total scores. Determine which group had the highest number of points, listing the words on the flip chart. Mark the longest word on this list; then record the longest word formed by each of the other groups.

Sample Words

Two letters:	ad, am, an, on, to, us
Three letters:	and, arm, bad, bed, bet, cot, cow, fan, has, ham, ire, jut, mar, net, pen, pie, sat, say, sin, ten, tow, toy
Four letters:	band, bare, bond, city, corn, crow, dare, dark, duty, farm, harm, mane, note, peat, pine, rise, suit
Five letters:	bared, bares, crisp, dread, noted, lease, spear
Six letters:	corner, darken, please, spread
Seven letters:	corners, darkens, leisure, picture, pleased, speared
Eight letters:	pictured, pictures, pleasure, surprise

Discussion

- What was the longest word formed by any group?
- Did your group have a strategy for the game? If so, what was it?
- How did time pressures affect your group's performance?
- How can we relate this activity to the way in which problems are solved in the workplace?

146

Boggled Worksheet

Rules: Each group member in turn contributes a word. To count, one letter in a word must be connected to a previous letter by a side or a corner and no letter may be "doubled." For example, at the top right, "TON" is an acceptable word, but "TOO" is not. However, once you pass from one letter to another, you may return to any previously used letter. For example, at the bottom left, "WOW" is an acceptable word.

Scoring: Each word is worth the *square* of the number of letters it contains. A two-letter word is worth four points (2 x 2) but a four-letter word is worth sixteen points (4 x 4).

H	M	A	F	T	O
A	R	N	E	B	N
E	S	P	K	D	A
N	I	J	U	R	E
R	C	T	I	S	P
W	O	Y	A	E	L

SCORE:

Two-letter words   _____ x 4 = _____

Three-letter words   _____ x 9 = _____

Four-letter words   _____ x 16 = _____

Five-letter words   _____ x 25 = _____

Six-letter words   _____ x 36 = _____

Seven-letter words   _____ x 49 = _____

Eight-letter words   _____ x 64 = _____

TOTAL POINTS = _____

Book Deal

Objective

To balance all members of a group on one book.

Time Required

Ten minutes.

Group Size

Five to thirty participants, who will work in groups of five.

Materials

One telephone directory for each group; stopwatch. (*Variations:* Several books.)

Preparation

None.

Process

1. Instruct the participants to form groups of five members each and to stand in a circle.

2. Place one telephone directory in the center of each group.

3. Explain that the objective is for each group to plan a method for all the members of the group to be supported off the floor by the book at the same time for a period of five seconds. Five minutes will be allowed for planning, during which time no trial, practice, or rehearsal is allowed. At the end of the planning period, each group will attempt to execute its plan without talking.

4. Signal for the planning process to begin. Time for five minutes, then stop the process.

5. Have each group, in turn, attempt to balance all members on the book for a period of five seconds. Remind the group members that no talking is allowed during the actual attempt.

Variations

1. Divide participants into two groups of equal numbers and direct each group to see how many of its members can be supported by one book.

2. Divide participants into two groups of equal numbers and ask each group to determine the least number of books necessary to support all of its members.

Discussion

- How successful was your group? Why?
- What could your group have done differently to improve its performance?
- How can we relate this activity to teamwork in general?

Boxed In

Objective

To predict the contents of a sealed box.

Time Required

Ten to fifteen minutes.

Group Size

Six to thirty participants, who will work in groups of three to five.

Materials

One copy of the Boxed In Worksheet, a pencil, one small box with cover, and three to six small weighted objects (in a variety of sizes, shapes, and materials) for each group; tape; clock or timer.

Preparation

Prepare one box for each group. After placing three to six weighted objects in the box, put the cover on, and tape the box securely so that access to the contents is prohibited.

Process

1. Instruct the participants to form groups of three to five members each.

2. Holding up one of the prepared boxes, tell the participants that the box contains a variety of different objects. Explain that each group will be receiving its own box and that group members will attempt to determine what items are contained in their respective boxes. They may shake the boxes, tilt them, listen to them, smell them, and so forth, as long as the lid is not removed during the process. Each group will have five minutes to discuss their observations and to come up with a "best guess" list of what is in the box.

3. Distribute one copy of the Boxed In Worksheet, a pencil, and one prepared box to each group.

4. Signal for the groups to begin their observations, timing the activity for five minutes. When time expires, stop the activity.

5. Proceeding in turn, direct each group to report its list of guessed objects, open its box, and then compare the actual objects against the predictions.

Discussion

- How accurate was your group's prediction?

- How did your group approach the task of guessing the objects in its box?

- What role does personal observation play in a person's ability to solve problems in the workplace?

Boxed In Worksheet

Directions: Try to determine what items are contained in your group's box. You may shake the box, tilt it, listen to it, smell it, and so forth, as long as the lid is not removed during the process. You will have five minutes to discuss your observations and to list your predictions of the box's contents below.

Comprehensive Coverage

Objective

To match proverbs that share a similar context.

Time Required

Ten to fifteen minutes.

Group Size

An unlimited number of participants, who will work in groups of three to five.

Materials

One copy of the Comprehensive Coverage Worksheet and a pencil for each participant; clock or timer.

Preparation

None.

Process

1. Instruct the participants to form groups of three to five members each, seated at separate tables.

2. Distribute one copy of the Comprehensive Coverage Worksheet and a pencil to each participant.

3. Explain that the worksheet lists a collection of proverbs in two columns. The seven proverbs on the left-hand side have numbers and the fourteen on the right-hand side have letters. Each numbered proverb has close application to *two* of the lettered statements. For example, Statement 1, "Every cloud has a silver lining," has a close relationship to Statement E, "It is a long lane that has no turning," as well as to one other statement. Group members are to match up the two letters, A through N, that correspond to each numbered proverb. Announce that groups will have five minutes to complete the task.

4. Signal for the activity to begin, then call time after five minutes. Referring to the Answers section below, review the answers with the group as a whole by obtaining feedback from the participants.

Answers

1. E and H
2. F and K
3. J and L
4. B and G
5. C and I
6. D and M
7. A and N

Discussion

- Were the proverbs difficult to understand? Why or why not?
- Select one of the proverbs, then describe what it means in your own words.
- Why can thoughts and ideas be communicated in many different ways? (*Individual experiences and background influence patterns of communication.*)
- How does this impact the communication process in general?

Comprehensive Coverage Worksheet

Directions: There are seven numbered proverbs on the left-hand side of this page and fourteen lettered ones on the right. Each numbered proverb shares a similar context with two of the statements from the right-hand column. For example, Statement 1, "Every cloud has a silver lining," has a close relationship to Statement E, "It is a long lane that has no turning," as well as to one other statement. For each number, match up *two* letters, A through N, and place them in the Answers section below.

1. Every cloud has a silver lining.
2. Anyone can hold the helm when the sea is calm.
3. They counsel best who live best.
4. More is obtained from one book carefully read than from libraries skimmed with a wandering eye.
5. They are truly wise who gain wisdom from the mishaps of others.
6. Cowards die many times before their death.
7. As for me, all I know is that I know nothing.

A. Wisdom is often nearer when we stoop than when we fly.
B. Jack of all trades, master of none.
C. Learn and profit by observing other people's experiences.
D. They who fear too much suffer more than those who die.
E. It is a long lane that has no turning.
F. Untempted virtue is easiest to keep.
G. Concentrate your energies for best results.
H. It's an ill wind that blows no good.
I. Learn to see in another's calamity the ills you should avoid.
J. A good example is the best sermon.
K. An unassaulted castle is easily defended.
L. Practice what you preach.
M. The valiant never taste of death but once.
N. The doorstep to the temple of wisdom is a knowledge of our own ignorance.

Answers:

1. __E__ and _____
2. _____ and _____
3. _____ and _____
4. _____ and _____

5. _____ and _____
6. _____ and _____
7. _____ and _____

Crossfire

Objective

To pass an object to other group members positioned alternately.

Time Required

Ten minutes.

Group Size

Sixteen to twenty-four participants, who will work in two groups of equal size. An even number of participants is required.

Materials

Two soft sponge balls or bean bags.

Preparation

None.

Process

1. Instruct the participants to form two groups of equal size and to remember who is in their group, identifying them in some way if necessary. The groups are to stand in two lines approximately three feet apart, facing one another. Next, direct every other member of each group to change places with the player opposite so that each player faces a member of the opposing group and has a member of the opposing group on either side.

2. Give a ball (or bean bag) to each group leader at one end of the two lines.

3. Explain that, on your signal, the leaders will begin passing the balls to the group members diagonally opposite (to members of their own groups), with each person in the group continuing this diagonal process. When a ball reaches the end of the line, it is to next pass back in the opposite direction until it reaches the group leader. This will complete *one pass*, as shown below. The object is to make *three* complete passes, with the ball reaching the original leader at the end of the third pass. Announce that the first group to complete passing the ball three times is the winner.

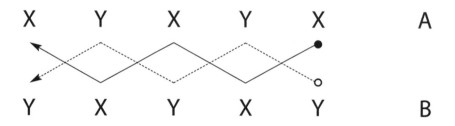

4. Signal for the groups to begin. Stop the activity when one group finishes three complete passes.

Discussion

- Was it difficult to perform the task? Why or why not?
- In what way(s) did the two balls "compete" with each other?
- How can we relate this activity to events in the workplace?

Disorderly Conduct

Objective

To rearrange eight sequential numbers so that no two consecutive numbers touch.

Group Size

Eight to forty participants, who will work in groups of eight. If there are extra participants after groups form, assign one or two additional members to each group.

Time Required

Ten minutes.

Materials

One set of number cards for each group; felt-tipped marker; flip-chart sheet; tape; clock or timer.

Preparation

Using eight 8½" x 11" card-stock sheets, write the numbers, 1, 2, 3, 4, 5, 6, 7, 8 (one per card) with the marker. Make one set for each group. Prepare the following chart on a flip-chart sheet and then display it:

```
            1

      2     3     4

      5     6     7

            8
```

Process

1. Instruct the participants to form groups of eight members each. (If there are extra participants after groups form, assign one or two additional members to each group.)

2. Distribute one set of number cards to each group. Direct the members of each group to each take one card and to hold it displayed in front of them.

3. Referring to the display chart, tell the members of each group to arrange themselves using the same configuration as shown.

4. Explain that each group member is to move to a new position so that no two consecutive numbers are together, whether side by side, up and down, or diagonally. Additional members of a group are to act as coaches. Announce that groups have approximately five minutes to complete the challenge.

5. Signal for the groups to begin, and time the activity for approximately five minutes. Stop the activity when time expires or all groups have completed the challenge, whichever occurs first.

Solution

```
            7

      3     1     4

      5     8     6

            2
```

Discussion

- How well did your group do in meeting this challenge?
- What approach did you take in trying to solve the problem?
- If you could do this activity again, what would you do differently?
- How can the choice of a specific technique influence a group's ability to solve workplace problems?

Fractured Phrase

Objective

To create new words from two smaller ones.

Time Required

Ten minutes.

Group Size

Five to thirty participants, who will work in groups of three to five.

Materials

One sheet of 8½" x 11" card stock and one envelope for each group; scissors; flip chart and felt-tipped marker; clock or timer.

Preparation

Duplicate the Fractured Phrase Cards page on card stock. Cut the sheet into twenty individual cards, then place them into an envelope. Prepare one envelope for each participating group.

Use the flip chart to record the words found in the Answers section below; keep the chart concealed.

Process

1. Instruct the participants to form groups of three to five members each.

2. Distribute one envelope containing the Fractured Phrase Cards to each group.

3. Explain that the envelope contains twenty three-letter words that can be arranged so as to produce ten six-letter words. The groups will have five minutes in which to complete the task.

4. Signal for the activity to begin and time it for five minutes. Stop the activity when time expires.

5. Referring to the prepared flip-chart sheet, reveal the correct answers.

Answers

BAR-TER	MAN-AGE	PER-SON
DON-KEY	NET-HER	SUN-KEN
FOR-MAT	PAR-ROT	TAR-GET
GOT-TEN		

Discussion

- How many of the six-letter words were you able to form?
- Why were some words more difficult to arrange then others?
- How willing were you to change your initial card combinations to find a more appropriate match?
- How does this relate to change management in general?

Fractured Phrase Cards

BAR	TER
DON	KEY
FOR	MAT
GOT	TEN
MAN	AGE
NET	HER
PAR	ROT
PER	SON
SUN	KEN
TAR	GET

Group Loop

Objective

To support a looped rope through balanced participation.

Time Required

Ten minutes.

Group Size

Eight to twenty participants.

Materials

Ten to fifteen yards of rope.

Preparation

Securely tie the two ends of the rope to form a large loop.

Process

1. Give the rope to the participants and have them step inside the loop. Instruct them to face center and space themselves equally, pulling the loop up behind them. Participants should step back and lean on the rope, stretching it taut enough to support everyone.

2. Next, divide the group into four separate subgroups. Direct two of the subgroups that face each other to release the rope and switch places, while the other two subgroups continue to stretch the rope to take up the slack.

3. Point out that, as the two subgroups reassemble and lean on the rope again, it will stretch and the other two will be drawn toward the center once again.

4. Direct the subgroups who did not move previously to repeat the process of switching places, while the other two subgroups stretch the rope.

5. Continue to repeat the procedure, alternating between the sets of facing subgroups, so as to set up a rhythm of switch and stretch.

Discussion

- Was it difficult to perform this task? Why or why not?
- Did the process improve over time? Why or why not?
- How can we relate this activity to teamwork in general?

Hand It Over

Objective

To pass a penny, from one end of a line to another, on the backs of group members' hands.

Time Required

Five minutes.

Group Size

Twelve to twenty-four participants, who will work in two equal-sized groups.

Materials

Two pennies.

Preparation

None.

Process

1. Instruct the participants to form two groups of equal size. Direct the members of each group to stand shoulder to shoulder, facing the other group. Choose a person at the end of each line to be the leader of his or her group.

2. Explain that the groups will be in competition to pass a penny from one end of the line to the other. Each leader will have a penny placed on the back of one hand. Upon a signal, the person will then transfer the penny to the other hand by placing the back of his or her hand over the penny and then flipping both hands at once. When the penny is on the back of the other hand, it must be passed to the next player using the same method. If a penny is dropped, it must be taken back to the beginning and the process must start over again. Use a penny to demonstrate the process. (*NOTE:* For smaller groups, you may want to have the groups complete a double pass of the penny in order to win.)

3. For each group leader, place a penny on the *back* of the person's hand closest to you. When both groups are ready, signal for the race to start.

4. Declare the first group that completes the penny pass as the winner.

Variation

The penny can be passed from one closed fist to another by placing the fist holding the coin, on end, over the top of the other person's fist, also on end, and then releasing the penny to be caught by the fist on the bottom.

Discussion

- What factors helped your group to perform the task?
- What hindered your group's progress?
- How can we relate this to teamwork in general?

Let's Get Cubical

Objective

To visualize a three-dimensional object from looking at a diagram on a flat surface.

Time Required

Ten minutes.

Group Size

An unlimited number of participants, who will work in groups of three or four.

Materials

One copy of the Let's Get Cubical Worksheet and a pencil for each participant; clock or timer.

Preparation

None.

Process

1. Instruct the participants to form groups of three to four members each.

2. Distribute one copy of the Let's Get Cubical Worksheet and a pencil to each participant.

3. Referring to the worksheet, explain that the object of the game is for group members to imagine what each option would look like when folded into a cube. They should then determine which of the four choices shown would fold up to form the cube presented at the top of the sheet. Groups will have three minutes in which to complete the task.

4. Signal for the groups to begin, then time the activity for three minutes. Give a one-minute warning before time expires, then stop the activity.

5. Obtain feedback from each group as to its selection; then reveal the solution given below.

Solution

Option "C."

Discussion

- How did you feel about working on this problem?

- What assumptions did your group need to make in order to solve this problem?

- How can we relate this type of problem solving to the workplace?

Let's Get Cubical Worksheet

Directions: Decide which of the choices below (A, B, C, or D) will fold up to form the cube presented here:

A.

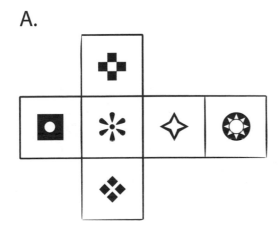

B.

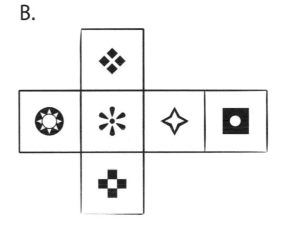

C.

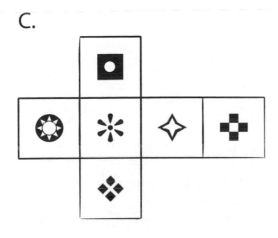

D.

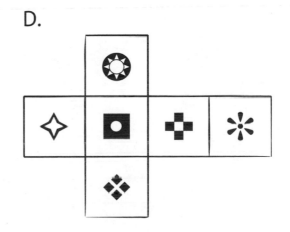

Numbers Game

Objective

To determine the answer to an equation from clues, the answers to which contain number references.

Time Required

Ten minutes.

Group Size

An unlimited number of participants, who will work in groups of three or four.

Materials

One copy of the Numbers Game Worksheet and a pencil for each group; clock or timer.

Preparation

None.

Process

1. Instruct the participants to form groups of three or four members each.

2. Distribute one copy of the Numbers Game Worksheet and a pencil to each group.

3. Referring to the worksheet, explain that there are five clues, the answers to which contain references to specific numbers. Groups are to find the answers to all five clues, then use the number from each answer in an equation to calculate a solution. Announce that groups will have five minutes to complete the task.

4. Signal for the activity to begin, then time it for five minutes. Give a one-minute warning before calling time.

5. Obtain the groups' answers and their solutions to the equation. Review the correct answers and solution, as given below.

Solution

A. 6-shooter

B. Sweet 16

C. 8-ball

D. 60 Minutes

E. 10-gallon hat

Answer: 54 $[6 \times (16 - 8)] + (60 \div 10)$

Discussion

- What factors influenced your group's performance on this task?
- How does this relate to group problem solving in general?

Numbers Game Worksheet

Directions: Each clue below describes a phrase that contains a reference to a number. Find the answers to all five clues, then use the number from each answer to calculate a solution to the equation shown at the bottom of the page.

A. A type of gun _____

B. Teen birthday milestone _____

C. Don't get behind this object _____

D. Popular expose TV show _____

E. Texas topper _____

$$[A \times (B - C)] + (D \div E) = ?$$

Answer: _____

Odd Man Out

Objective

To locate the one item in a grouping that does not belong with the others.

Time Required

Ten minutes.

Group Size

An unlimited number of participants, who will work in groups of three or four.

Materials

One copy of the Odd Man Out Worksheet and a pencil for each participant; flip chart and felt-tipped marker; stopwatch or clock.

Preparation

Write the following suggested answers and reasons on a flip-chart sheet and conceal the sheet prior to the session.

1. viola   only stringed instrument.
2. darts   not played with a ball

3. meringue   only sweet food

4. mammal   not a specific breed

5. Egypt   word does not contain letter A

6. pirouette   name of step not dance

Process

1. Instruct the participants to form groups of three or four members each.

2. Explain that each group member will receive a worksheet listing groups of items. Say that one item in each listing does not belong with the others. Groups will have exactly three minutes to locate the item that does not belong in each of the six groupings and to specify the reasons for their choices.

3. Distribute one copy of the Odd Man Out Worksheet, face down, and a pencil to each group member.

4. Signal for groups to begin the activity. Time for exactly three minutes, then stop the activity.

5. Referring to the prepared flip-chart sheet, review the suggested answers and reasons for each of them. Determine whether any group had different answers and or reasons, checking them for appropriateness. Poll the groups for the number of listings they were able to complete.

Discussion

- Did your group work together or was the task divided among members?
- How well did your group do?
- What role did time pressure play in your performance?
- How do these factors influence group problem solving and decision making in the workplace?

Odd Man Out Worksheet

Directions: Circle the "odd man out" in each of the following groups, then explain your reasoning.

1	flute	clarinet	viola	bassoon	piccolo

Reason:

2	squash	tennis	baseball	darts	table tennis

Reason:

3	ragout	minestrone	moussaka	meringue	kebab

Reason:

4	monkey	mongoose	tiger	elephant	mammal

Reason:

5	Lapland	Egypt	Canada	France	Zambia

Reason:

6	tango	pirouette	waltz	foxtrot	black bottom

Reason:

Rope Trick

Objective

To list a variety of solutions to resolve a problem.

Time Required

Ten to fifteen minutes.

Group Size

Six to thirty participants, who will work in groups of three to five.

Materials

One copy of the Rope Trick Worksheet, a sheet of newsprint paper, and a felt-tipped marker for each group; clock or timer; tape or push pins.

Preparation

None.

Process

1. Instruct the participants to form groups of three to five members each.

2. Distribute one copy of the Rope Trick Worksheet, a sheet of newsprint paper, and a felt-tipped marker to each participating group.

3. Explain that the groups have been presented with a unique problem. Read the following aloud:

> Two ropes are hanging vertically from a wall, reaching down to waist level. You want to hold onto both of them at the same time, but there is too much distance between the ropes and your reach is too short. What do you do?

Using the newsprint sheet, each group is to list at least seven possible solutions to resolve this problem. Announce that groups will have five minutes to complete the task.

4. Signal for the groups to begin, then time the activity for five minutes. Stop the groups when time has expired.

5. Direct each group, in turn, to post its sheet and present its list of solutions to the large group. Present some of the solutions below, if not already identified.

Possible Solutions

Call someone to help you.

Hold one rope and grab the other one with your toes.

Lengthen one rope with a piece of string.

Tie a stick to the end of one rope to make it longer.

Swing on one of the ropes.

Set one rope swinging, then grab the other.

Nail one rope to the wall first.

Discussion

- What was the total number of different suggestions generated by all the groups combined?

- Were similar solutions identified by more than one group? Which were they?

- What were some of the more creative ideas?

- Why is it important to think "outside the box" when solving some problems?

Rope Trick Worksheet

Instructions: Your group has five minutes in which to find at least seven different ways to resolve the following problem.

Two ropes are hanging vertically from a wall, reaching down to waist level. You want to hold onto both of them at the same time, but there is too much distance between the ropes and your reach is too short. What do you do?

Switchback

Objective

To compete in a cooperative tug of war.

Time Required

Ten minutes.

Group Size

Twelve to twenty participants, who will work in two equal-sized groups.

Materials

Rope (approximately twenty to thirty feet in length); tape; felt-tipped marker; clock or timer.

Preparation

Mark the center point of the rope with the marker. Using the tape, mark a one-foot line on the floor. Lay the rope on the floor perpendicular to the line, with its center point resting on the tape.

Process

1. Instruct the participants to form two equal-sized groups. Have the two groups line up on opposite sides of the line on the floor in a tug-of-war formation.

2. Assign numbers to the different players on each side of the rope; that is, for twenty participants, 1 through 10 on one side and 1 through 10 on the other side as well.

3. Explain that the groups will engage in a tug-of-war competition. However, whenever a number is called, the players on each side having that number must trade places. All the other players must keep on pulling with all their strength while the crossover is taking place. The winning group will be the one that has the middle mark of the rope on its side of the taped mark on the floor at the end of five minutes.

4. Direct the groups to pick up the rope and begin pulling on your signal. Signal to start, and time the activity for five minutes. During this time, randomly announce a number approximately every forty-five to sixty seconds. Stop the activity when time expires.

Variation

When a number is called, instead of changing places with the other group, have the appropriate group members perform a specific task, such as face backward, move to the front or back of the line, remove a shoe, and so forth, for the remainder of the activity.

Discussion

- How did you feel about switching groups during the competition?
- How does this relate to managing change?
- How does this relate to the concept of "cooperative competition"? (*One must rely on interdependence with other groups to provide necessary resources, even when groups compete to be the best.*)
- How does this activity relate to managing change in general?

Variation Discussion

- How did you feel about being singled out to do something different?
- Did the changes affect your group's ability to perform? Why or why not?
- How does this relate to the ability of group members to coordinate their efforts?

Symbol Explanation

Objective

To determine the numerical values of a series of patterns.

Time Required

Ten to fifteen minutes.

Group Size

An unlimited number of participants, who will work in groups of three or four.

Materials

One copy of the Symbol Explanation Worksheet and a pencil for each group; flip chart and felt-tipped marker; clock or timer.

Preparation

Using the worksheet as a reference, prepare a flip-chart sheet with the following four symbols: burst, square, star, and diamond.

Process

1. Instruct the participants to form groups of three or four members each.

2. Distribute one copy of the Symbol Explanation Worksheet and a pencil to each participating group.

3. Explain that the numbers on the worksheet represent the sums of the values in each row or column. Group members are to use the patterns represented on the chart to determine the numerical values for X and Y. Announce that groups will have five minutes to complete the task.

4. Signal for group work to begin, timing for five minutes. Stop the activity when time expires.

5. Ask participants for feedback to determine the value for each symbol in the chart: the burst, the square, the star, and the diamond. Record each value next to the appropriate symbol on the prepared flip-chart sheet. Obtain the corresponding values for X and Y and record these on the flip chart.

Solution

X = 22 and Y = 25. Each burst equals 1, a square equals 5, the star equals 10, and a diamond equals 2.

Discussion

- Did your group find the correct values? Why or why not?
- How well did members of your group work together?
- What process did your group use to approach the problem?
- How does this activity relate to problem solving in the workplace?

Symbol Explanation Worksheet

Directions: Use the pattern represented in the chart below to determine the value for X and Y. Your group will have five minutes to complete the task.

8-pointed star	square	5-pointed star	square	21
square	8-pointed star	5-pointed star	diamond	18
5-pointed star	5-pointed star	square	5-pointed star	35
square	5-pointed star	square	square	Y =
21	26	30	X =	

Taking Care of Business

Objective

To form a list of words derived from letters in a phrase.

Time Required

Ten minutes.

Group Size

An unlimited number of participants, who will work in groups of three to five.

Materials

One copy of the Taking Care of Business Worksheet and a pencil for each participant; flip chart and felt-tipped marker; clock or timer.

Preparation

None.

Process

1. Instruct the participants to form groups of three to five members each.
2. Distribute one copy of the Taking Care of Business Worksheet and a pencil to each participant.
3. Explain that each group will work together for approximately five minutes to list as many different words as possible, utilizing the letters found in the phrase:

TAKING CARE OF BUSINESS.

To form a word, participants may use each letter only as many times as it is contained in the actual phrase; that is, only one "T" may be used, but it is possible to use the letter "S" three times.

4. Signal for the activity to begin. Stop the activity after approximately five minutes.
5. Determine which group had the longest list of words. Obtain feedback from each group and make a composite list of the various words on a flip chart.

Variation

Use your organization's name or the name of a department or division within the company to form words that describe positive qualities.

Discussion

- Did your group make effective use of its resources (available letters)? Why or why not?
- What could your group have done differently?
- How can you relate this activity to adaptation to change in the workplace?

Taking Care of Business Worksheet

Directions: Utilizing letters from the phrase below, list as many different words as possible. To form any word, you may use each letter only as many times as it appears in the actual phrase; for example, you may use only one "T," but the letter "S" may be used three times in a word.

TAKING CARE OF BUSINESS

Tell-Tale Time

Objective

To determine the logical time sequence for a series of clocks.

Time Required

Ten minutes.

Group Size

An unlimited number of participants, who will work in groups of three or four.

Materials

One copy of the Tell-Tale Time Worksheet and a pencil for each group; clock or timer.

Preparation

None.

Process

1. Instruct the participants to form groups of three or four members each.

2. Distribute one copy of the Tell-Tale Time Worksheet and a pencil to each group.

3. Referring to the worksheet, explain that the clocks displayed in the first series follow a strange sort of logic. The challenge is for each group to determine what time the fourth clock should show, stating the reasoning at the bottom of the sheet. Announce that the time limit for the task is five minutes.

4. Signal for group work to begin, and time for five minutes. Give a one-minute warning, then stop the groups when time expires.

5. Obtain feedback from each group as to the answer and reason. Reveal the correct answer (see below) and reasoning.

Answer

Option A.   *Reasoning:* At each stage the *big* hand moves *counter-clockwise,* first by ten minutes, then twenty, and finally, by thirty minutes; at the same time, the *small* hand moves *clockwise,* first by one hour, then two hours, and finally, by three hours.

Discussion

- Did your group determine the correct answer? Why or why not?
- What problem-solving steps did your group make?
- How well did members of your group work together?
- What does this activity show about working together on the job?

Tell-Tale Time Worksheet

Directions: The clocks below follow a strange sort of logic. Your group's challenge is to determine what time the fourth clock should show. You will have five minutes to complete the task.

?

Choose from these four options by circling the appropriate letter. State your reasoning below.

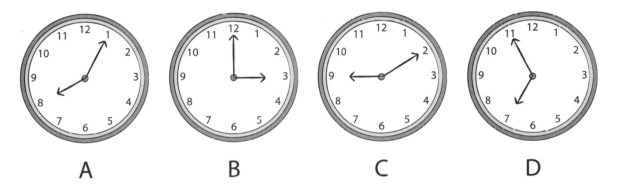

A   B   C   D

REASONING:

Treasured Memories

Objective

To re-create a treasure map from memory.

Time Required

Fifteen minutes.

Group Size

Six to twenty participants, who will work in groups of three or four.

Materials

One copy of the Treasured Memories Map, one sheet of paper, and a pencil for each group; the prepared Treasured Memories Map and a cover sheet for the facilitator; clock or timer.

Preparation

Draw a Treasured Memories Map of an imaginary island and indicate on it a variety of landmarks (trees, mountains, lakes, rivers, roads, and so forth), as well as pirate symbols (skull and crossbones, gold ingots, kegs of rum, barrels of flour, muskets, and so forth). Also mark an "X" to indicate where the buried treasure is waiting to be found.

Process

1. Instruct the participants to form groups of three or four members each. Distribute one sheet of paper and a pencil to each group.

2. Explain that everyone will have an opportunity to view a map for two minutes. Then each group will be asked to draw the map from memory, including its shape and everything marked on it.

3. Cover the Treasured Memories Map with a sheet of paper, then place it on a table. Invite the participants to gather around the table. Once everyone is in place, uncover the map and allow the participants to look at it for exactly two minutes. When time is up, cover the map.

4. Direct the participants to return to their groups. Tell them that each group is to re-create the map from memory—its shape and everything marked on it. Group members will have five minutes in which to complete the task.

5. Allow approximately five minutes for group work, then call time. Have each group, in turn, share its version of the map, pointing out the marked treasure spot ("X"). Ask the groups to vote on which of the maps they feel is the most accurate.

6. Distribute one copy of the Treasured Memories Map to each group. Allow the groups a few minutes to compare their maps with the original.

Variation

Allow only one person from each group to view the map. The group representative will then return to his or her group and verbally describe the map to the remaining members, who will draw the picture.

Discussion

- How close was your group's map to the original one?
- What causes discrepancies between what we see and what we remember?
- How does this impact day-to-day situations in the workplace?

Ups and Downs

Objective

To solve visual puzzles that relate to the words "up" and "down."

Time Required

Fifteen minutes.

Group Size

An unlimited number of participants, who will work in groups of three to five.

Materials

One copy of the Ups and Downs Worksheet and a pencil for each participant; clock or timer.

Preparation

None.

Process

1. Instruct the participants to form groups of three to five members each. Have each group select a group recorder.

2. Distribute one copy of the Ups and Downs Worksheet and a pencil to each participant.

3. Explain that group members are to work together to identify the familiar saying represented by each visual puzzle on the Ups and Downs Worksheet. Announce that groups will have approximately ten minutes to solve the puzzles.

4. Signal for the activity to begin. Allow approximately ten minutes, then call time.

5. Using feedback from the groups and the Answers stated below, review the saying revealed by each puzzle.

Answers

(1) A big letdown.
   (LET in thick letters going downward.)

(2) Split right down the middle.
   (SPLIT along right margin + DOWN in the middle.)

(3) Down and out.
   (AND going downward + EXIT indicating a way out.)

(4) One-upmanship.
   (ONE going upward + symbol for man + abbreviation for ship Queen Elizabeth 2)

(5) Time's up.
   (Time designations AM and PM going upward)

Variation

As a pre-workshop or break-time activity, have each participant work on the puzzles individually and review the answers at the end of the session.

Discussion

• Did your group use the title of the worksheet as a clue for solving the puzzles? Why or why not?

• How did perception play a role in solving these puzzles?

• How can puzzles like these help stimulate creative problem solving?

Ups and Downs Worksheet

Directions: Identify the familiar saying represented by each visual puzzle that follows.

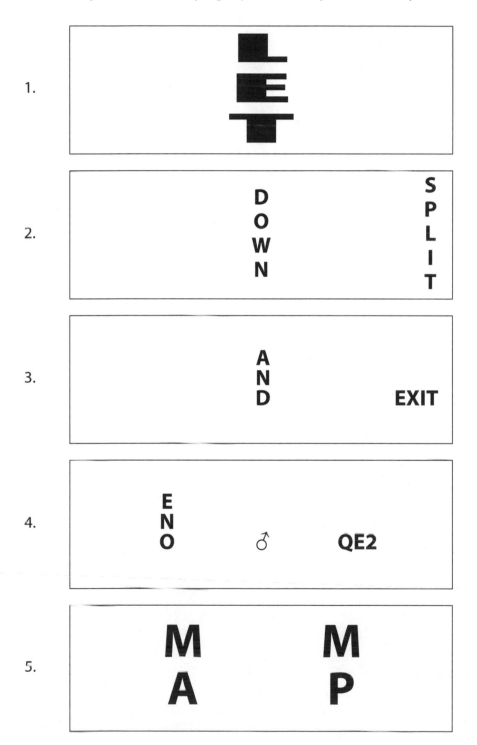

1.

2.

3.

4.

5.

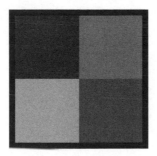

About the Author

Lorraine L. Ukens is the owner of Team-ing with Success, a consulting and training enterprise specializing in team building and leadership development. Her wide range of business experience, spanning more than twenty years, is applied in designing, facilitating, and evaluating programs in a variety of human resource development areas. Lorraine, an adjunct faculty member in the HRD graduate program at Towson University in Maryland, is the author of several training books and games, including *Getting Together: Icebreakers and Energizers* (Jossey-Bass/Pfeiffer, 1997), *Working Together: 55 Team Games* (Jossey-Bass/Pfeiffer, 1997), and *All Together Now! A Seriously Fun Collection of Interactive Training Games and Activities* (Jossey-Bass/Pfeiffer, 1999). She received her M.S. degree in human resource development from Towson University and is an active member of the American Society for Training and Development at both the national and local levels.

Lorraine L. Ukens

Adventure in the Amazon

Activity and Leader's Guide

In this exciting activity, participants face a simulated "jungle survival." They must reach agreement in this imaginary setting in order to succeed, and they learn why consensus produces the best decisions.

When their plane makes an emergency landing in the jungle, participants need to decide which of 15 items on the plane—including tallow candles, a pistol, safari hats, and other objects—would be most essential to their survival. Participants experience synergy as never before!

Use this gripping simulation to:

- *Improve* decision-making skills
- *Enhance* problem-solving abilities
- *Strengthen* group cooperation . . . and much more!

No one wants to write a team "pep talk" that could fall flat. Human resource professionals, team leaders, and managers will want to conduct this refreshing activity with their groups and teams in any work setting.

Activity / 16 pages • Leader's Guide / 16 pages
••••••••••••••••••••••
Adventure in the Amazon Activity
Item #F451

Leader's Guide
Item #F450

Lost at Sea

Simulation and Leader's Manual

In this classic simulation, participants work individually then as a group to assess fifteen items salvaged from a yachting accident, based on their value for survival. Results are compared with the expert rankings supplied by the U.S. Merchant Marines. The *Leader's Manual* offers instructions for facilitating the activity.

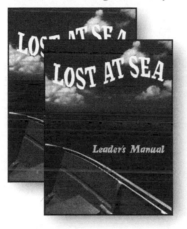

In this simulation, a group is stranded on a rubber life raft with minimal supplies including:

- Fishing kit
- Mosquito netting
- Shark repellant
- Shaving mirror
- Two chocolate bars
- And ten other items

TIMING
1½ hours

AUDIENCE
Work teams—4 to 9 team members may participate at one time—several groups may be directed simultaneously

---

Simulation / 7 pages • Leader's Manual / 10 pages
••••••••••••••••
Lost at Sea Simulation
Item #B630

Leader's Manual
Item #B494

Spark synergy in an icy wasteland!

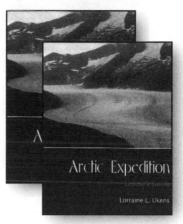

Lorraine L. Ukens

Arctic Expedition

Activity and Leader's Guide

Activity participants embark on a simulated journey through a frozen, forbidding landscape, and experience team synergy as they never dreamed possible.

Any work setting is suitable for conducting this activity. Your facilitator, who does not need to be a training professional, will need a copy of the *Leader's Guide*, which contains detailed instructions about running the simulation. Each participant needs a copy of the *Activity*, the guidebook to this exhilarating experience.

In this icy wasteland, leaders will spark a synergy that sets teams afire!

TIMING
1½ hours

AUDIENCE
Work teams with 4 to 9 members; several teams may be directed simultaneously

---

Activity / 16 pages • Leader's Guide / 16 pages
••••••••••••••••
Arctic Expedition Activity
Item #F448

Leader's Guide
Item #F447

Even Trainers Need Training!

Karen Lawson

Train-the-Trainer

Facilitator's Guide and The Trainer's
Handbook

Facilitator's Guide

The demand for training often exceeds the available
resources. That's when organizations turn to their
subject-matter experts. These employees often have
no training experience, but they have valuable information to share with
their coworkers.
Usually, these sub-
ject-matter experts
are given little or no
formal instruction
on how to train. It's
sink or swim. They
struggle to convey their expertise, and their untu-
tored training can fall on unwilling ears.

> **Remember—even trainers need
> training! Build a solid foundation
> for new trainers with this "total-
> trainer" development workshop
> and resource guide.**

The *Train-the-Trainer* workshop is the helping
hand that no new trainer can do without. The
Instructor's Guide gives you the tips, tools, checklists,
and guidelines you need to conduct an effective,
interactive train-the-trainer program.

You'll teach new trainers how to:

- *Conduct* a needs assessment
- *Identify* their training style
- *Design* their instructional plan
- *Use* active training techniques
- *Deliver* their training
- *Evaluate* their training . . . and much more!

Plus, this guide is packed with figures and
exhibits you'll use as overheads, flip charts, and
handouts. And the *Train-the-Trainer* workshop is

flexible: • the full program is 6 days, but if time and
money are limited, you can shorten the program
• the modules can be delivered on consecutive days,
or they may be distributed over several weeks. Pick
and choose! If your audience won't have any respon-
sibility for conducting a needs assessment, the mod-
ular design of the *Train-the-Trainer* workshop allows
you to eliminate the needs assessment section from
the program. You'll have no problem making this
comprehensive program suit your training schedule!

The Trainer's Handbook

The Trainer's Handbook is a component of the workshop and a stand-alone resource. Both novice and
pro trainers—even if they haven't participated in the
workshop—will find this handbook indispensable!

New trainers will learn the basics, plus they'll get practical tips on:

- *Assessing* the attitudes of your participants
- *Keeping* your training learner-centered
- *Remaining* sensitive to the diversity of your
  audience
- *Incorporating* games into your training
- *Selecting* audio-visual aids
- *Closing* your sessions creatively . . . and more!

Facilitator's Guide / looseleaf / 300 pages • The Trainer's
Handbook / paperback / 240 pages

• •

Train-the-Trainer Facilitator's Guide
Item #F469

The Trainer's Handbook
Item #F470

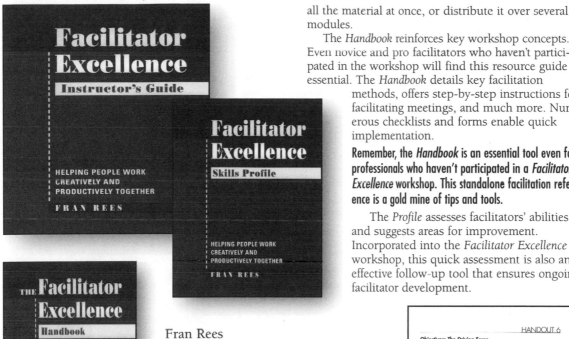

all the material at once, or distribute it over several modules.

The *Handbook* reinforces key workshop concepts. Even novice and pro facilitators who haven't participated in the workshop will find this resource guide essential. The *Handbook* details key facilitation methods, offers step-by-step instructions for facilitating meetings, and much more. Numerous checklists and forms enable quick implementation.

Remember, the *Handbook* is an essential tool even for professionals who haven't participated in a *Facilitator Excellence* workshop. This standalone facilitation reference is a gold mine of tips and tools.

The *Profile* assesses facilitators' abilities and suggests areas for improvement. Incorporated into the *Facilitator Excellence* workshop, this quick assessment is also an effective follow-up tool that ensures ongoing facilitator development.

Fran Rees
Facilitator Excellence

Instructor's Guide, Handbook, and Profile

Today's organizations are using teams to carry out tasks and solve problems. To get the job done, your managers and team leaders need to communicate and cooperate. Facilitation is the skill that saves the day! This workshop shows your employees how to become effective facilitators, and enables them to develop this skill in others. Great facilitators promote employee commitment and satisfaction, and augment team performance and problem solving. And flawless facilitation starts with *Facilitator Excellence*.

The *Instructor's Guide* includes everything you need to conduct a facilitation workshop: simulations, discussion resources, and more. The flexible workshop is organized around practical problems, so participants never lose sight of the job. You can deliver

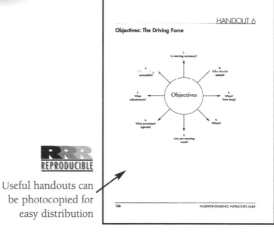

Useful handouts can be photocopied for easy distribution

This package helps professionals to:

- *Lead* meetings effectively
- *Organize* team activities
- *Obtain* project support
- *Find* solutions to problems
- *Establish* harmony among coworkers
- *Deal* with customers and clients
- *Set* goals and make decisions
- *Earn* support for initiatives . . . and much more!

You'll need one copy of the *Instructor's Guide* for the trainer, skilled facilitator, or manager who will conduct the workshop. Each participant will need one copy of the *Handbook* and the *Profile*.

Instructor's Guide / looseleaf / 256 pages • Handbook / paperback / 240 pages • Profile / 16 pages

• • • • • • • • • • • •

Instructor's Guide
Item #F318

Handbook
Item #F319

Profile
Item #F320

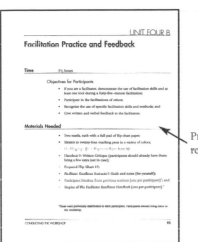

Practical activities reinforce material
